Have Your Cake and Eat It

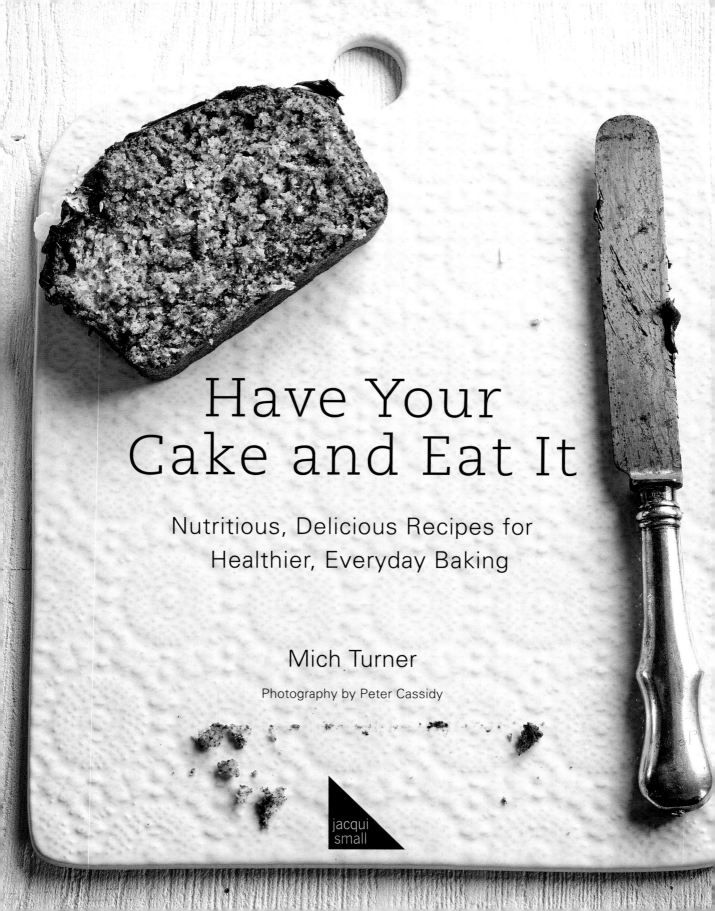

Have Your
Cake and Eat It

Nutritious, Delicious Recipes for
Healthier, Everyday Baking

Mich Turner

Photography by Peter Cassidy

jacqui
small

Publisher Jacqui Small
Managing Editor Emma Heyworth-Dunn
Project Manager and Editor Abi Waters
Art Director Penny Stock
Photographer Peter Cassidy
Props Stylist Rebecca Newport
Production Maeve Healy

ISBN: 978 1 911127 16 1

A catalogue record for this book is available from the British Library.

2019 2018 2017

10 9 8 7 6 5 4 3 2 1

Printed in China

First published in 2017 by Jacqui Small LLP, 74–77 White Lion Street, London N1 9PF

Quarto is the authority on a wide range of topics.
Quarto educates, entertains and enriches the lives of our readers – enthusiasts and lovers of hands-on living.
www.QuartoKnows.com

Contents

NUTRITION TAG KEY
Specific nutrition qualities
are highlighted on relevant
recipes to provide an at-a-
glance snapshot of important
nutrition benefits.

GF gluten free

DF dairy free

F good source of fibre

LF lower fat

EF egg free

Introduction

Baking brings a huge amount of pleasure to those who are baking, those who are receiving, and those who are sharing – but it can be a minefield to know what to bake and how to bake successfully so you can enjoy eating cake without feeling guilty.

I made my very first wedding cake 30 years ago, and have made, baked and decorated over 10,000 cakes since then. I have always said a cake should be a feast for the eyes and a memory for the palate. As a qualified food scientist, former bakery and patisserie buyer, industry consultant and TV judge I never tire of innovation – adapting recipes and formulating new ones to find the very best, most delicious, nutritious recipes to bake, present and share.

In this book I want to give you choices. I am a strong advocate of using ingredients in season, with provenance and the very best quality for maximum flavour and texture. It is so true that a cake can only be as good as its ingredients and subtle changes can dramatically enhance and alter the characteristics of a bake.

I have included recipes with added nutrition, such as fresh and dried fruits, nuts and seeds, featuring alternatives for gluten, fats, sugars and dairy to accommodate your personal diet and lifestyle. Ultimately, every recipe has to be delicious and I will guide you through the different baking skill levels from complete novice to experienced baker – offering practical tips and hints to ensure each and every cake is baked to success.

This book is not intended as a health or diet book. I do use butter, sugar and cream, but I will steer you through the nutritional benefits and comparisons of these ingredients and recipes, giving you options so you can choose which cakes to bake for which occasion.

I have included gluten free, dairy free, fat free, lower fat, lower sugar, lighter, more nutritious recipes that are in no way bland or boring.

This book is for those who like to bake or who aspire to be able to bake and for those who like to eat or would like to eat cake in moderation and with the knowledge that it is as nutritious and wholesome as possible.

Ingredients

It is a fact that a cake can only be as good as the ingredients you use. However, the good news is a bake can be improved and enhanced with the careful selection and inclusion of delicious and nutritious ingredients. As a qualified food scientist and nutritionist I hope to expel some myths and highlight the nutritional benefits of many ingredients used in this book to help you have your cake and eat it.

Cakes and bakes are essentially made up of carbohydrate or starch (such as flour to absorb the moisture and set the structure); eggs to bind, stabilize and aerate; fat to carry the flavour, provide mouthfeel and improve the keeping qualities; and sugar, which adds sweetness.

Within these categories there are many variations that will play a pivotal role, and there are many other additions such as fresh or dried fruits, vegetables, nuts, spices and chocolate from nature's own bounty to enhance your bakes and add nutritional benefit.

It is important to remember that these bakes should be included as part of a wider healthier diet and not consumed in total isolation!

LEFT Frozen fruits can be used to make a fabulous fruit compote out of season. Add orange zest for added flavour.

Fats

Fats can be derived from vegetable or animal sources and yield the highest amount of energy – 9 calories per gram.

The body can synthesize most of the fats it needs from the diet. However, there are two essential fatty acids, linoleic and alpha-linoleic acid, that cannot be synthesized and must be ingested from food. These essential acids are so called because they are required for normal, healthy function of many biological processes including mood enhancers, reducing inflammation and healthy nerve function. A lack of essential fatty acids could lead to dermatitis and poor skin healing. There is also evidence that low levels or an imbalance of these essential fatty acids may be a factor in osteoporosis. Sources of these essential fatty acids include linseed (flaxseed), olive oil, soya oil, canola (rapeseed) oil, chia seeds, pumpkin seeds and sunflower seeds.

Fats can be trans, saturated, monounsaturated or polyunsaturated. Mono- and polyunsaturated fats are fats found in nuts, nut butters, seeds and seed oils to provide essential fatty acids and fat-soluble vitamins A,D, E and K. They can be consumed in smaller quantities where they help to maintain healthy cholesterol levels.

Saturated fats include butter, whole milk, cream and coconut oil. They are more stable when heated than other fats and should be consumed in moderation as they can increase the amount of cholesterol in the diet.

Trans fats include hard vegetable margarines and hydrogenated vegetable oils. The process of hardening oils to be solid at room temperature turns them from an unsaturated to a saturated fat. The structure of the fat created (trans) is harmful to the body increasing the LDL cholesterol.

By making and baking your own cakes and biscuits you can be aware of the fats in your diet – opting to include more polyunsaturated essential fatty acids, limiting saturated fats and avoiding trans fats altogether.

Fats include:
Butter
Sunflower, olive, canola, soya oil
Vegan spread
Coconut oil
Nut butters – peanut, cashew, almond, hazelnut
Cream cheese
Double cream
Whipping cream
Soured cream
Greek yogurt
Coconut milk
Buttermilk
Cow's milk
Soya milk
Egg yolk

SUNFLOWER OIL

Sunflower oil is 100 percent vegetable fat and is suitable for vegans, vegetarians and those following a gluten-free, dairy-free diet. It works well in batter cakes or those made by the melted method as it is liquid at room temperature, which helps to keep the cake moist. Look for high-quality cold-pressed or organic sunflower oil.

COCONUT OIL

Coconut oil is 100 percent saturated fat, but contains mid-length triglycerides that are thought to provide better health and nutritional benefits. Coconut oil contains no cholesterol and is a good choice for a non-dairy diet.

Coconut milk

Peanut butter

Cream cheese

Greek yogurt

Double cream

Buttermilk

Sunflower oil

Coconut oil

Unsalted butter

Vegan margarine

BUTTER

Made from churning cow's cream, butter must contain a minimum of 80 percent fat. It is a saturated fat, but not a trans fat, therefore it is more stable when heated and can be metabolized in the body. I use unsalted butter in all my baking, which offers a fresh, creamier, distinctive flavour that is not salty. Salted butter will have a longer shelf life as salt is a preservative. Butter contains calcium as well as fat soluble vitamins.

VEGAN MARGARINE OR SPREAD

To be used successfully in baking, look for vegetable margarines that contain a minimum of 80 percent fat. Avoid spreads as they will affect your baking. Look specifically for a NON-TRANS fat, as these oils have to be hydrogenated in some way to be solid at room temperature.

COCONUT MILK

Made by soaking grated coconut flesh in hot water. Coconut milk is rich in fibre, water-soluble B vitamins and minerals including iron, selenium, sodium, calcium, magnesium and phosphorous for healthy metabolism and bones. Unlike cow's milk, coconut milk does not contain lactose and can be used by those following a lactose-free or dairy-free diet.

PEANUT BUTTER

An excellent source of protein, fibre and B vitamins as well as iron and potassium. Both crunchy and smooth, nut butters are sources of saturated and unsaturated fats. Made by crushing the roasted nuts to a paste. Be sure to choose the no added salt or sugar varieties.

CREAM CHEESE

A soft cheese made from cream and milk, usually with a stabilizer such as locust bean gum added. It is 34 percent fat, providing 342 calories per 100g (3½oz) and 110mg cholesterol per 100g (3½oz). At 34 percent fat versus the 80 percent fat of butter, cream cheese frostings can offer a good lower fat frosting.

GREEK YOGURT

Full-fat Greek yogurt contains just 9 percent fat and 116 calories per 100g (3½oz). It should be live or bio – offering beneficial microflora and no added sugar. Lower or 0 percent fat yogurts will have less fat soluble vitamins, may have added sugar and will be less creamy and lack flavour.

DOUBLE CREAM

This type of cream is 48 percent fat and can be boiled, whipped or frozen. Always be careful when whipping double cream – it can be overwhipped very easily, turning grainy and eventually splitting into butter and buttermilk. Extra thick double cream is recommended for spooning or serving as the cream has been homogenized (the fat globules have been evenly distributed).

WHIPPING CREAM

This is a lighter version of double cream with a fat content of over 35 percent – the minimum amount necessary to allow it to stay firm once beaten or whipped. The fat globules encase the air and when whisked, provide the characteristic texture of whipped cream. Whipping cream whips well and can be used for pouring.

SOURED CREAM

A single cream (20 percent fat) that's been soured using an added culture (similar to that used in yogurt). It is not suitable for whipping so I use it to fill cakes or in frostings.

BUTTERMILK

This is the liquid that remains after the butter has been separated from milk or cream. With only 40 calories per 100g (3½oz) and less than 1 percent fat I tend to use buttermilk in scones as the lactic acidity in the buttermilk activates the raising agent.

Flours & Carbohydrates

Carbohydrates provide 4 calories per 100g (3½oz) but, more importantly in baking, offer structural support to baked cakes. The starch granules swell during the baking process until they burst and absorb the liquid. As baking continues, the starch sets and the baked cake will stabilize. Correct temperature, accurate measurements and adhering to baking times will help ensure that cakes are baked correctly.

Wheat flour contains the proteins glutenin and gliadin. When these come into contact with liquid they form the elasticated protein gluten responsible for achieving the lift in bakes and breads. Many people choose to avoid gluten if they have a food intolerance or feel better when limiting or excluding it from their diet. For those suffering from coeliac disease, which is an autoimmune disease, gluten must be avoided.

Other grains such as rye, oats and barley also contain gluten – in lower quantities.

Many carbohydrates, other than the obvious wheat flour, can be used in baking. These include:
Plain flour (gluten)
Wholemeal flour (gluten)
Spelt flour (lower gluten)
Gluten-free flour
Polenta
Cornflour
Popping corn
Oats (lower gluten)
Gluten-free oats
Pinhead oatmeal
Ground almonds
Cocoa powder

FLOURS
Barley & spelt flours (an ancient variety of wheat) can be substituted in part for wheat flour to add texture and flavour, but are less readily available, and will give different results as they are lower in gluten.

Wholemeal flour contains all of the wheat grain and offers additional nutrition. This flour works well in melted method cakes, where there is a lot of moisture and strong flavours from spices and sugars. Cakes made with wholemeal flour tend to be more dense, with less aeration, and require more moisture before baking; but can offer a greater depth of flavour and texture.

Cornflour is used very much as a thickening agent in baking. It is ground from the dried maize and is gluten free.

Wheat flour provides the best result for cakes – light, aerated with sufficient starch and protein to support the cake and absorb the moisture during baking. Cakes should be made with all-purpose wheat flour, which is lower in gluten and never with strong bread flour, which is much higher in gluten and will result in tough, chewy, dense cakes.

Plain flour is pure wheat flour with no raising agents added.

Self-raising flour has baking powder already included in the flour.

Gluten-free flour can be milled from rice, corn, tapioca, buckwheat or potato and can be substituted successfully in cake baking where the recipe requires a lower percentage of flour by design, and has other strong flavours included – such as chocolate, spices or treacle. The effect of using gluten-free flour tends to be more crumbly

Popcorn

Oats

Ground almonds

Pinhead oatmeal

Coconut flour

Polenta

Spelt

Wholemeal flour

Cornflour

Self-raising flour

Plain wheat flour

Gluten-free flour

with a gritty texture and stronger aftertaste. Xanthan gum can be added to cakes made with gluten-free flour to improve the crumb structure and reduce crumbling.

Coconut flour is gluten free and high in fibre with a distinctive, earthy flavour. I tend to use it in conjunction with wheat flour rather than by itself otherwise the bakes can be quite dry.

POPCORN
Popping corn is added to a pan of hot oil. The kernels expand and puff up until the pressure builds sufficiently to create a 'pop' and popcorn is created. Gluten free and containing lots of air, 100g (3½oz) kernels will go a long way and provide 382 calories with just 4g fat. The kernels are a notable source of B vitamins and iron.

POLENTA
Polenta is gluten-free ground corn or maize. It is less than 1 percent fat, with 0 percent cholesterol. It offers a wonderfully grainy texture to bakes.

PINEAD OATMEAL
Pinhead oatmeal, steel-cut oats or oat groats are the inner kernel of the whole oats, which have been roughly chopped, offering a chewier, nutty-flavoured oat.

OATS
Oats are generally considered healthy as they are a good source of protein, fibre and B vitamins. They offer slow release energy and thanks to their beta glucans have been proven to lower cholesterol.

GROUND ALMONDS
Made from ground sweet blanched almonds. Gluten free and rich in polyunsaturated fats.

RAISING AGENTS & CHEMICALS
These raising agents go hand in hand with the carbohydrates and can be obtained as gluten-free varieties.

Bicarbonate of soda is a powerful chemical raising agent that reacts with acids such as vinegar, buttermilk, yogurt or lemon juice to produce carbon dioxide, which will lift the bakes. It works well with batter cakes and stronger flavours.

Baking powder is a more gentle raising agent for softer, lighter, more subtle flavoured cakes.

Cream of tartar stabilizes egg whites increasing their heat resistance and maximizing volume when making meringues or chiffon-style cakes.

Vinegar reacts with bicarbonate of soda to produce carbon dioxide as a powerful raising agent. It must be used as soon as they are mixed.

Sugars

Sugars have come in for some negative press in light of their link to obesity, Type 2 diabetes, cardiovascular disease and tooth decay. Sugars and syrups are necessary for baking in whatever guise you choose. They are all processed similarly within the body, requiring insulin produced in the pancreas to maintain a sugar balance in the blood.

Be sensible; use natural sources of sugar derived from fruits and dairy products, which will add nutritional benefits of fibre, vitamins and minerals and thereby will enable you to reduce the added sugars. Be aware of the refined versus unrefined sugars. Offering no difference in nutritional value, the unrefined sugars will have enhanced flavour and trace elements that you will notice the flavour more, rather than just being sweet. Some recipes, however, will benefit from the refined sugar, visually – and I have clearly highlighted these so you can choose to use alternatives if you wish. Encourage yourself to enjoy the flavour of your bakes rather than the sweetness.

Sugar offers 4 calories per gram and can be categorized into monosaccharides, disaccharides and oligosaccharides. Monosaccharides are the simplest of sugars and include glucose, galactose and fructose (fruit sugar). Disaccharides include sucrose, also known as common table sugar, such as granulated, caster and icing sugar (made up of glucose and fructose monosaccharides) and lactose (milk sugar – made up of glucose and galactose monosaccharides). Oligosaccharides are made up of chains of these simple sugars and are found in many fruits and vegetables.

Sugars include:

Golden icing sugar

Icing sugar

Demerara sugar

Granulated sugar

White caster sugar

Golden caster sugar

Soft light brown sugar

Soft dark brown sugar

Muscovado sugar

Glucose syrup

Maple syrup

Honey

Golden syrup

Treacle

Molasses

Jam

Citrus curds (see page 18)

Fruit compote (see page 19)

The main difference between white and brown (raw) sugar is that the brown (raw) sugar hasn't been completely refined. This raw brown sugar will contain a small percentage of molasses with trace amounts of the minerals calcium, potassium, iron and magnesium. The darker the sugar the more molasses the sugar will contain – between 5–10 percent. The molasses add to the colour and flavour, from caramelized through to treacle flavour.

TOP TIP

The body metabolizes carbohydrates into simple sugars. The brain uses glucose as its sole energy source. A good reason to eat cake!

Molasses sugar

Maple syrup

Treacle

Dark muscovado sugar

Honey

Molasses

Demerara sugar

Light soft brown sugar

Granulated sugar

Golden syrup

Golden caster sugar

White caster sugar

Golden icing sugar

White icing sugar

Glucose syrup

Citrus Curds

Citrus curds, using fresh lemon, lime, orange or passion fruit are great by themselves or stirred into buttercreams for a zesty filling. These work really well injected into cupcakes and muffins for extra flavour, texture and colour.

 GF

ALL CURDS MAKE ABOUT 550–600G (19–21OZ)

FOR LEMON CURD

4 lemons, rind and juice

350g (12oz) golden caster sugar

4 eggs, beaten

100g (3½oz) unsalted butter, chilled and cubed

FOR ORANGE CURD

1 large orange, rind and juice

juice of 2 lemons

275g (9¾oz) golden caster sugar

3 eggs, plus 1 egg yolk, beaten

100g (3½oz) unsalted butter, chilled and cubed

FOR PASSION FRUIT CURD

8 passion fruits, cut in half and flesh and seeds scooped out

juice of 1 lemon

225g (8oz) golden caster sugar

3 medium eggs, plus 1 egg yolk, beaten

90g (3¼oz) unsalted butter, chilled and cubed

FOR LIME CURD

2 limes, rind and juice

2 medium lemons, rind and juice

225g (8oz) golden caster sugar

3 medium eggs, plus 1 egg yolk, beaten

90g (3¼oz) cubed unsalted butter

1 Place the citrus rind or passion fruit flesh and seeds in a saucepan together with the juice, sugar, eggs and butter. Heat over a medium-low heat stirring all the time. Do not let the curd boil. As it gradually thickens it will begin to coat the back of a wooden spoon.

2 Remove from the heat and strain through a fine metal sieve.

Store for up to 4 weeks in clean jars in the refrigerator.

 TOP TIPS

- The curd should be heated until it thickens to ensure the eggs are hot enough to cook the curd, making it safe and stable.
- Do not let the curd boil as this will damage the delicate protein structure of the eggs and the curd will scramble and be rubbery.
- Blending the eggs really well before adding them helps to stabilize.

Fruit Berry Compote

Fresh fruit berry compotes are a natural inclusion to add flavour, interest, texture and nutrition to your bakes. They can be stirred into cake batters before baking; added to buttercreams to naturally colour and flavour; spread between layers or onto meringues and pavlovas; or injected into muffins and cupcakes for a fruity hit.

Use fruits as they are in season or frozen berries throughout the year. As the fruits are heat treated and combined with sugar, they will keep for up to 14 days in the refrigerator, and can be frozen in small containers for up to 3 months. Defrost thoroughly before using.

 GF DF

MAKES ABOUT 500G (18OZ)

400g (14oz) fresh or frozen fruit (strawberries, raspberries, blackcurrants, blackberries)

100g (3½oz) golden caster sugar

grated zest and juice of 1 lemon or orange (optional)

1 Place the fruit, sugar and citrus zest and juice, if using, together in a heavy-based saucepan over a medium heat and bring to a gentle simmer. Continue to heat, stirring occasionally for about 25–30 minutes until the fruit has softened and reduced to a thick pulp.

2 Remove from the heat. Taste and adjust the sugar or add lemon juice to taste.

Store for up to 14 days in an airtight container in the refrigerator.

 TOP TIP
The fruit should simmer gently but not be a rolling boil as it could burn and damage the flavour of the fruit.

Other Ingredients

In order for my bakes to have added nutrition and be utterly delicious, I have chosen to include nature's best ingredients in the form of nuts, seeds, spices, fruit and vegetables.

FRUIT
Fresh, dried or frozen, there is an abundance of fruit that can be used in baking to provide natural sweetness, fibre, vitamins, minerals, flavour, texture and colour. Many dried fruits will provide a concentrated source of these nutrients to have a significant benefit to boosting the daily intake of essential vitamins and minerals.

Dried fruits include apricots, prunes, figs, dates, raisins, cherries, cranberries, sultanas and currants. Make sure you choose unsweetened varieties.

Fresh fruits include berries, apples, pears, pineapple, bananas, peaches, plums, nectarines, apricots and the citrus fruits. Choose fruits as they are in season and buy local when you can.

Frozen fruits are a great choice for fruit compotes. They can be easily stored and used any time throughout the year. They are picked and frozen when they are most ripe, usually making them a less expensive and more convenient way to obtain these summer berries.

FRESH VEGETABLES
Carrots, pumpkins, beetroot, parsnips and courgettes can be used in baking to add moisture, dietary fibre and nutritional vitamins and minerals to cakes. They are generally lower in simple sugars and have much less, if any, fat.

NUTS
All nuts can be used in baking to add protein, essential fats, minerals and vitamins as well as high energy, flavour

and texture. Roasting the nuts beforehand can intensify the flavour and crunch by driving off some of the oil. Always use fresh and avoid salted nuts. My favourites include cashews, almonds, walnuts, pecans, pine nuts, hazelnuts, macadamias and pistachios. They are often interchangeable so experiment to find your favourites.

SEEDS

Pumpkin, sunflower, chia, linseed and poppy seeds will provide powerful energy, antioxidants, essential oils and vitamins and minerals. A little go a long way and offer an alternative to nuts. Add a handful to bakes, crumbles, loaf cakes and muffins to boost the overall nutritional content.

SPICES

Fresh root ginger has a wonderful mellow, fragrant and distinctive flavour that can enhance many cakes and bakes. Spices such as cinnamon, nutmeg and all spice are all good store cupboard staples.

VANILLA

The most versatile natural flavour is vanilla – taken from the root of the vanilla orchid plant. The seeds have a distinctive and potent flavour and come in a variety of forms for convenience in your bakes – from vanilla pods, powder, extract and paste. Be sure to choose the real thing and avoid vanilla flavour or flavouring.

EGGS

An essential ingredient in baking. The egg white (albumen) is an elasticated protein that provides aeration to bakes. When used at room temperature, the egg white can create a honeycomb structure of air sacs like thousands of tiny balloons all together. The warmer the egg white, the more it can expand, the more air sacs and ultimately the more air into

your cakes – leaving them super light and aerated. Rushing or using cold eggs will inhibit the amount of air that can be incorporated and the bakes will not be as light and aerated as they could be.

Egg yolk contains a powerful emulsifier – lecithin. This emulsifier will stabilize an emulsion (water and oil) creating stable bakes.

Eggs are delicate structures, they like to be added slowly and like to be warm. They act as a binding agent and offer protein, essential fats and nutrients. A word of caution though – egg yolk is very high in cholesterol – one large egg yolk contains approximately 180mg cholesterol. The recommended daily allowance is 300mg (200mg if you are considered high risk).

Chocolate

Chocolate is produced from fermenting, drying, cleaning and roasting cocoa beans. Once the shell is removed, the cocoa nibs are ground to cocoa mass. This mass is liquefied into cocoa solids and cocoa butter.

I generally use a dark chocolate with 70 percent cocoa solids – this is made primarily of cocoa solids and cocoa butter with very little added sugar and no added milk. This chocolate has added nutritional benefits of fibre, iron, magnesium, copper, manganese, potassium, phosphorus, zinc and selenium and can be appropriate for those following a dairy-free diet.

The fat in this dark chocolate may have a beneficial effect on cholesterol levels as it consists mainly of stearic and oleic acid. While stearic acid is a saturated fat, it is unlike other saturated fats as it does not raise blood cholesterol levels. Oleic acid is a monounsaturated acid which does not raise cholesterol levels and may even reduce it.

Dark chocolate & cocoa contain powerful antioxidants to protect against ageing, cardiovascular disease and encourage cell regeneration.

Semi-sweet chocolate is a combination of cocoa solids, cocoa butter (or possibly vegetable fat) and sugar.

Milk chocolate will have the addition of milk powder or condensed milk and not suitable for those following a dairy free diet.

White chocolate contains cocoa butter, sugar and milk but none of the beneficial cocoa solids.

The lower the cocoa solids, the greater the sugar and added fat and fewer beneficial nutritional effects.

Drinking chocolate contains primarily sugar with cocoa powder, salt and flavouring. The cocoa solids are usually around 25 percent. I have only used this in my recipe to dust the Chocolate-dusted Orange Madeleines (see page 52).

Cocoa

Drinking chocolate

Milk chocolate

Dark chocolate

White chocolate

51% semi-sweet chocolate

Cake dos and don'ts

As a food scientist I am aware of the physical chemistry when I am making and baking cakes. To become a better baker, it helps to understand what to do and why you are doing it.

FRESH INGREDIENTS
It is imperative you use the freshest ingredients of the highest quality. Buy fresh, use fresh and don't compromise.

WEIGH ACCURATELY
Baking is a science relying on delicate interactions between ingredients. Invest in a set of digital scales, and measuring spoons to accurately measure all dry and wet ingredients. Don't rely on guesswork and annotate any changes you make to a recipe so you can remember for another time.

TEMPERATURE
Most ingredients work best at room temperature – including butter, sugar, flour and eggs. Butter will cream better and eggs will whisk better. Take the ingredients out of the refrigerator the night before you are intending to bake. Don't be tempted to warm butter in the microwave – it will just melt and then not be suitable for creaming. Eggs will pasteurize when the temperature reaches between 61–70°C (142–158°F). Invest in a digital thermometer to accurately measure temperature to ensure eggs and syrups are safe and stable.

PREHEATING THE OVEN
Preheat the oven to the correct temperature before placing the bakes in the oven. This will ensure the batter quickly reaches the desired temperature to achieve the physical changes necessary during baking. Too low and the cake ingredients will melt before being baked resulting in a soggy, sunken, pale cake. Too high and the cake surface and sides will colour, burn and dry out long before the centre of the cake is baked. Use oven gloves to protect yourself in the kitchen.

CORRECT UTENSILS
- Use the right tool for the task.
- Beating and creaming should be with a wooden spoon or electric hand or desktop mixer fitted with a beater attachment.
- Folding should be done with a metal spoon or rubber blade spatula.
- Whisking should be with a balloon hand whisk or electric hand or desktop mixer fitted with a whisk attachment.
- Graters, microplanes, zesters, peelers, rubber spatulas, scissors and knives will all help maximize your ingredients and bakes.

CORRECT SIZED TINS & LINING
Measure tins to ensure you are using the size stated in the recipe. This will ensure the batter fits the tin and bakes according to the recipe. Line tins with non-stick baking parchment, melted butter or not at all (e.g. for chiffon cakes)

UNDERSTAND THE PHYSICAL CHEMISTRY TERMINOLOGY
Rubbing in – combining fat with dry ingredient, either with your fingertips (if you have cold hands) or with an electric mixer fitted with a paddle attachment. The idea is not to melt the butter as it is distributed in small granules through the dry ingredient.

Creaming – beating the fat and sugar together to create a light, aerated emulsion. It is not possible to over-cream – so turn the electric mixer on and leave it on for a good 10 minutes.

Folding – carefully distributing the dry ingredients into an emulsion or batter. Use a metal spoon or rubber spatula to avoid knocking out air or overworking the gluten in the flour. Both would result in a dense, tough, chewy cake.

Beating – blending ingredients together but not necessarily to aerate. Use a wooden spoon or electric mixer fitted with a paddle attachment.

Melting – the process of turning a solid to liquid.
- Butter – melt in the microwave or in a small saucepan over a medium heat.
- Chocolate – melt in a bowl suspended over a pan of gently simmering water or in a bowl in the microwave with medium heat being careful not to burn the chocolate.

Whisking – using a hand or electric whisk. The act of adding air to cream or eggs to achieve a highly aerated foam. Avoid fat or grease in the bowl. Wash in hot soapy water, rinse and dry with absorbent kitchen towel.
- Eggs can be whisked to a frothy, soft peak or firm peak stage.
- Cream should be carefully whipped and not be granular.
- Eggs and sugar for whisking or meringues should be light, even and frothy, with a velvety appearance.

Caramelizing versus burning – sugar will pass through a series of changes from light thread syrup to black jack as it heats from 100 to 200°C (212 to 392°F). Heat slowly and carefully.

PATIENCE
The most important quality to be a successful baker is patience. Allow yourself plenty of time to make a cake – perfection cannot be rushed and understanding all these principles will ensure you develop into a successful, confident baker.

SUGAR TEMPERATURES

NAME	TEMPERATURE	TOUCH / VISUAL TEST	USE
Syrup	100°C (212°F)	Coats a spoon	Basic stock syrup – as used in vanilla cake
Soft ball	115–116°C (239–240°F)	Forms a soft ball when rolled	Jams and jellies – fruit compote
Firm ball	118–120°C (244–248°F)	Forms a firm ball when rolled	Italian meringue
Hard ball	124–128°C (255–262°F)	Forms a hard ball that holds its shape	Marshmallows
Soft crack	130–132°C (266–269°F)	Will not roll and will show small cracks as sets	Candies
Crack	135–138°C (275–280°F)	Will not form a shape and will crack when manipulated	Candies, soft nougat
Hard crack	146–155°C (295–311°F)	Will shatter when placed in water	Poured or pulled sugar nougat
Light caramel	155–160°C (311–320°F)	Visually a light amber	Praline
Caramel	160°C (320°F)	Dark brown	Praline
Black jack	190–200°C (374–392°F)	Black and smoking	Burnt!

Muffins, Cupcakes & Buns

Probably the easiest entry level when it comes to baking, as you don't need to invest in a huge amount of equipment, time and skill to achieve fantastic baked results. These are a great and fun way to inspire beginners and children – to learn about ingredients, the baking process, flavours, textures and decoration. I have included scones, madeleines, friands and cupcakes to stretch your imagination and skill, and have been mindful of dietary requirements to offer you healthier choices for everyday baking.

Date, Banana & Peanut Butter Muffins

MAKES 12 MUFFINS

500g (1lb 2oz) ripe mashed
　bananas (about 4 large
　bananas)

125ml (4fl oz) sunflower oil

1 teaspoon vanilla bean paste

125g (4½oz) crunchy peanut
　butter

1 egg, beaten

350g (12oz) plain flour

125g (4½oz) soft light brown
　sugar

1 teaspoon baking powder

1 teaspoon bicarbonate of soda

225g (8oz) chopped dates or figs

3 tablespoons mixed sunflower
　and pumpkin seeds, plus extra
　for sprinkling

These delicious dairy-free cakes are baked in individual muffin cases so they are perfectly portioned. Relatively low in fat, the flavour is all in the banana, with texture from the peanut butter, dates and seeds. They are nutritious and wholesome with natural sugar, high fibre, vitamins and nutrients in the dried fruits, nuts and seeds. I like to have a batch of these available for mid-morning second breakfasts – they are also great for school or office packed lunches.

1 Preheat the oven to 180°C/gas 4. Line a muffin tin with 12 tulip muffin cases.

2 Mash the bananas in a large bowl with the sunflower oil, vanilla bean paste, peanut butter and beaten egg.

3 In a separate bowl, stir together the flour, sugar and raising agents. Add the chopped dates or figs and seeds and toss to coat.

4 Tip the flour into the banana mixture and stir until just combined.

5 Divide the batter between the 12 muffin cases and sprinkle with seeds. Bake for 20 minutes until golden. Leave to cool for 5 minutes before transferring to a wire rack.

Store for 2–3 days in an airtight container in the refrigerator. Not suitable for freezing.

These muffins are packed with fresh peach and raspberries and injected with fruit compote for natural added sweetness and flavour. They are dairy free – making them the perfect choice for breakfast or a mid-morning snack.

Peach Melba Muffins

MAKES 12 MUFFINS

210g (7½oz) plain flour

40g (1½oz) ground almonds

1 teaspoon baking powder

125g (4½oz) golden caster sugar

2 eggs

90ml (3fl oz) sunflower oil

250g (9oz) soya or coconut yogurt

2 large peaches, 1 stoned and
 chopped and 1 cut into
 12 slices

8 amaretti biscuits, lightly
 crushed

½ quantity Fruit Compote
 (see page 19), blended until
 smooth

50g (1¾oz) fresh raspberries

40g (1½oz) flaked almonds

1 Preheat the oven to 180°C/gas 4. Line a muffin tin with 12 cases.

2 Sift the flour, ground almonds and baking powder into a bowl.

3 In a separate bowl, mix together the sugar, eggs, oil and non-dairy yogurt. Add the flour and mix until just combined. Lightly fold in the chopped peach and crushed amaretti biscuits. Spoon the batter into the cases.

4 Spoon the smooth fruit compote into a piping bag and snip the end to make a small hole. Insert the tip just under the surface of the batter and inject about 2 teaspoons compote per muffin. Top with a peach slice, a few raspberries and some flaked almonds.

5 Bake for 25–30 minutes before cooling on a wire rack.

Store for 2–3 days in an airtight container in the refrigerator. Not suitable for freezing.

VARIATION
If using coconut yogurt, consider substituting the ground almonds with desiccated coconut.

4

MUFFINS, CUPCAKES & BUNS

LEFT 'Keeping You Regular' Muffins with prunes, apricots and figs.
RIGHT 'Back to Your Roots' Muffins with carrot, parsnip and beetroot.

Porridge, figs, apricots and prunes in a muffin – these will certainly help to keep you regular! Full of iron, B vitamins and fibre, these muffins are super quick to make and will easily keep hunger at bay. I have used sunflower oil and buttermilk, added texture with the hazelnuts and rounded the muffins off with a little cinnamon. Enjoy for breakfast or weekend brunch.

'Keeping You Regular' Muffins

MAKES 8 MUFFINS

175g (6oz) self-raising flour

50g (1¾oz) porridge oats

125g (4½oz) light muscovado sugar

2 teaspoons ground cinnamon

½ teaspoon bicarbonate of soda

1 large egg, beaten

150ml (5fl oz) buttermilk

1 teaspoon vanilla extract

90ml (3fl oz) sunflower oil

80g (3oz) chopped and roasted hazelnuts

60g (2¼oz) chopped prunes

60g (2¼oz) chopped apricots

60g (2¼oz) chopped figs

1 Preheat the oven to 180°C/gas 4. Line a muffin tin with 8 cases.

2 Put the flour, oats, sugar, cinnamon and bicarbonate of soda in a large bowl. Stir until well mixed.

3 In a separate bowl, mix together the egg, buttermilk, vanilla and oil. Stir into the dry ingredients to make a smooth batter. Set aside 30g (1¼oz) of the chopped hazelnuts and then fold in the chopped dried fruits and remaining hazelnuts.

4 Spoon the batter into the prepared cases and sprinkle over the reserved hazelnuts. Bake for 20–25 minutes. Serve warm or cold.

Store for 2–3 days in an airtight container at room temperature. Suitable for freezing.

Root vegetables have their own natural sweetness and contain no fat. Carrots, parsnips and beetroot can all be used, depending on your personal preferences and seasonal availability. These vegetables add fibre, flavour, texture, colour, vitamins and minerals and are nature's own harvest. Because they contain so much water they help keep the muffins nice and moist. I have made these dairy free and added coconut, with a little coconut flour to reduce the overall gluten content. Coconut flour is gluten free, absorbs a huge amount of water (which needs to be taken into account when using it in baking) and adds a gritty, rounded flavour.

'Back to Your Roots' Muffins

MAKES 12 MUFFINS

125g (4½oz) plain flour

50g (1¾oz) coconut flour

2 teaspoons ground cinnamon

1 teaspoon ground nutmeg

1 teaspoon mixed spice

1 teaspoon bicarbonate of soda

2 large eggs

150ml (5fl oz) sunflower oil

150g (5½oz) soft light brown sugar

grated zest of 1 orange

grated zest of 1 lemon

200g (7oz) grated root vegetables (a mixture of peeled carrots, beetroot, parsnip)

50g (1¾oz) chopped hazelnuts

1 Preheat the oven to 180°C/gas 4. Line a muffin tin with 12 cases.

2 Sift the flours together with the spices and bicarbonate of soda in a large bowl. Stir until well mixed.

3 In a separate bowl, beat together the eggs, oil and sugar until smooth. Stir in the dry ingredients and mix to a smooth batter.

4 Fold in the remaining ingredients. Spoon the batter into the prepared cases. Bake for 25–30 minutes, then leave to cool on a wire rack.

Store for 2–3 days in an airtight container at room temperature. Suitable for freezing.

Raspberry, Rose & Pistachio Cupcakes

The delicate flavour, colour and texture of these cupcakes marry beautifully to create cakes that I think are perfect for bridal or baby showers. Making mini cupcakes that are packed full of flavour and texture rather than regular size will allow every guest to sample a cake without the calorific content. Freeze-dried fruit powders add an intense flavour and sherbet fizz to the buttercream without adding moisture or the need for extra sugar or artificial colours.

**MAKES 18 REGULAR-SIZED OR
48 MINI CUPCAKES**

450g (1lb) fresh raspberries
(or enough for 3 raspberries
to be put in the base of each
cupcake liner)

250g (9oz) unsalted butter,
softened

250g (9oz) golden caster sugar

4 large eggs

250g (9oz) self-raising flour

½ teaspoon baking powder

60ml (2fl oz) whole milk

1–2 teaspoons rose water

75g (2¾oz) roughly chopped
pistachios

roasted and chopped pistachios
(see page 94), to decorate

FOR THE BUTTERCREAM

250g (9oz) unsalted butter,
softened

500g (1lb 2oz) icing sugar

2 tablespoons milk

3–4 teaspoons freeze-dried
raspberry powder

1 Preheat the oven to 170°C/gas 3. Place 18 cupcake liners in
cupcake tins (or 48 mini cupcake liners in mini cupcake tins) and
place 3 raspberries in the base of each (only use 1 raspberry if
using mini cupcake liners).

2 In a large bowl, cream together the butter and sugar. Add the
eggs, slowly, mixing until light and fluffy. Sift the flour and baking
powder into the batter and fold in carefully. Stir in the milk, rose
water and finally, the pistachios.

3 Fill a large piping bag with the batter, snip the end and pipe the
batter into the cupcake cases until they are two-thirds full. Bake
for 15 minutes until risen and golden brown. Remove from the
oven and transfer to a wire rack to cool.

4 To make the buttercream, whip the butter for 1–2 minutes
until soft. Add the icing sugar in 2 batches and whisk until fully
combined. Add the milk and raspberry powder and whisk. Top
each cupcake with a swirl of buttercream and decorate with
chopped roasted pistachios.

Store for 2 days in an airtight container at room temperature. Not
suitable for freezing.

1

3

These vegan cupcakes contain no dairy, eggs or honey. When eggs were rationed, cakes relied on a chemical reaction between vinegar and bicarbonate of soda to produce carbon dioxide, which would help lift the cakes during baking. This principle works in these vegan cupcakes that are decorated with a vegan frosting.

Vegan Vanilla Cupcakes

MAKES 12 REGULAR-SIZED OR 18 SMALLER CUPCAKES

300g (10½oz) golden caster sugar

150ml (5fl oz) sunflower oil

1 tablespoon vanilla bean paste

500g (1lb 2oz) dairy-free soya yogurt or a mix of soya, almond and coconut yogurt

2 teaspoons white spirit vinegar

360g (12¼oz) plain flour

1 teaspoon bicarbonate of soda

1½ teaspoons baking powder

toasted coconut flakes, for sprinkling

FOR THE VEGAN VANILLA BUTTERCREAM

300g (10½oz) vegan or non-dairy spread (at least 80% fat)

600g (1lb 5oz) golden icing sugar

1 tablespoon vanilla bean paste

1 Preheat the oven to 170°C/gas 3. Line a muffin tin with 12 cases (or a mini muffin tin with 18 cases).

2 Put the sugar, oil and vanilla in a large bowl and beat until well mixed. Blend the yogurt and vinegar together, then add to the bowl and mix well.

3 Sift together the flour, bicarbonate of soda and baking powder and add these to the cupcake batter. Stir until everything is mixed, then divide the batter between the cupcake cases until they are two-thirds full.

4 Bake for 20 minutes until risen and golden, then leave to cool on a wire rack.

5 To make the buttercream, beat the vegan spread for 1–2 minutes, then add the icing sugar in 2 batches. Add the vanilla bean paste to taste. Top each cupcake with a swirl of buttercream and decorate with toasted coconut flakes.

Store for 2–3 days in an airtight container in the refrigerator. Not suitable for freezing.

VARIATION
VEGAN CHOCOLATE CUPCAKES – substitute 2 tablespoons of the plain flour with cocoa powder and decorate with dairy-free chocolate buttercream (see below) and dairy-free dark chocolate decorations. DAIRY-FREE CHOCOLATE BUTTERCREAM – heat 110g (4oz) dark chocolate with 75ml (2¾fl oz) water until melted and smooth, then mix into 1 quantity of the vanilla buttercream (see above).

The Hummingbird cake originates from Jamaica and is named after the island's national bird. It is by nature a dairy-free cake with the added nutritional benefits of pineapple, bananas and nuts. It is usually layered with cream cheese frosting. The recipe was created and published internationally as a marketing strategy to encourage tourists to visit the island. I love the tropical, sunshine flavours and have chosen to use a dairy-free coconut frosting.

Hummingbird Cupcakes

MAKES 20 CUPCAKES

360g (12¼oz) plain flour

400g (14oz) golden caster sugar

1 teaspoon bicarbonate of soda

1 tablespoon ground cinnamon

260g (9¼oz) sunflower oil

3 large eggs, beaten

1 tablespoon vanilla bean paste

4 medium or 2 large very ripe bananas (about 450g/1lb)

225g (8oz) fresh or canned pineapple, crushed or finely chopped

100g (3½oz) chopped pecans or walnuts

edible flowers, to decorate

FOR THE DAIRY-FREE COCONUT FROSTING

230g (8¼oz) coconut oil

500g (1lb 2oz) icing sugar

25g (1oz) desiccated coconut

grated zest of 1 lime

1 Preheat the oven to 180°C/gas 4. Line two 12-hole muffin tins with 20 cupcake liners (or you can bake in batches).

2 In a large bowl, combine the flour, sugar, bicarbonate of soda and cinnamon. In a separate bowl, combine the oil, eggs and vanilla. Stir into the dry ingredients.

3 Mash the bananas and add them to the batter, along with the pineapple and pecans. Stir with a wooden spoon until just combined.

4 Spoon the batter into the cupcake liners until they are two-thirds full and bake for about 20 minutes until firm to the touch and a knife inserted in the centre comes out clean. Remove from the oven and transfer to a wire rack. Leave to cool in the tin for 5 minutes before turning out and leaving to cool completely.

5 To make the frosting, place the coconut oil in a suitable bowl and microwave for 30 seconds or until melted. Beat in the icing sugar in 2 batches until smooth and the right consistency. Stir in the desiccated coconut and lime zest to taste.

6 Top the cupcakes with a swirl of coconut frosting and decorate with edible flowers.

Store for 2–3 days in an airtight container at room temperature. Not suitable for freezing.

VARIATION
Alternatively, this batter will make 4 x 20cm (8 inch) round layers, which can be sandwiched together to make one large layered gateau.

Pumpkin Cupcakes with Cream Cheese Frosting and sprinkled with pecan praline.

Pumpkin Cupcakes with Cream Cheese Frosting

MAKES 12 CUPCAKES

225g (8oz) self-raising flour

1 teaspoon bicarbonate of soda

1 teaspoon ground ginger

1 teaspoon ground cinnamon

150ml (5fl oz) sunflower oil

150ml (5fl oz) soured cream

225g (8oz) soft light brown sugar

2 large eggs

125g (4½oz) canned pumpkin
    purée

75g (2¾oz) chopped pecans

1 quantity of Cream Cheese
    Frosting (see page 134),
    made with the addition of
    1 teaspoon ground cinnamon

1 quantity of Praline (see page
    134) to decorate, made with
    50g (1¾oz) toasted pecans
    and 100g (3½oz) caster sugar
    (optional)

Muffins and cupcakes are a great introduction to baking. With the added benefit of antioxidant rich, fibre rich, naturally sweet pumpkin these are also a great way to get more vegetables into the daily diet.

1 Preheat the oven to 200°C/gas 6. Line a 12-hole muffin or cupcake tin with paper cases.

2 Sift together the flour, bicarbonate of soda, ginger and cinnamon. In a separate bowl, mix together the oil, soured cream, light brown sugar, eggs and pumpkin purée. Add the wet ingredients to the dry and stir well. Stir in the pecans.

3 Spoon the muffin batter into the prepared cases until two-thirds full. Bake for 15–20 minutes until well risen and golden brown.

4 Leave to cool on a wire rack before topping with the cinnamon flavoured Cream Cheese Frosting and decorate with Pecan Praline, if using.

Store for 2–3 days in an airtight container in the refrigerator. Suitable for freezing.

TOP TIP
The praline will produce more than is required. Blitz one-third of the praline to a fine powder in a food processor and sprinkle it over the frosting. Roughly chop the remainder with a knife and decorate each cupcake.

VARIATION
Substitute the canned pumpkin purée with freshly grated pumpkin.

Friands are small oval cakes, originating from France. They are popular as a lighter muffin-style cake made with ground almonds, egg whites and icing sugar. They have less butter and flour and therefore less calories and fat than regular muffins. They are surprisingly easy to make and can be flavoured with fruits, spices, citrus zests, coconut, nuts or chocolate. I add blueberries as the tart acidity of the berries marries beautifully with the sweet cake beneath.

'You've Got a Friand in Me' – Blueberry Friands

MAKES 12 FRIANDS

200g (7oz) unsalted butter, melted and cooled, plus extra for greasing

250g (9oz) golden icing sugar

50g (1¾oz) plain flour

170g (6oz) ground almonds

6 medium egg whites (about 210g/7½oz)

grated zest of 1 orange

150g (5½oz) blueberries

30g (1¼oz) flaked almonds

1 Preheat the oven to 180°C/gas 4. Generously grease 12 friand moulds.

2 Sift the icing sugar and flour into a bowl. Add the ground almonds and mix well.

3 In a separate bowl, whisk the egg whites to a soft foam. Make a well in the centre of the dry ingredients and tip in the egg whites, orange zest and melted butter. Stir to form a soft batter.

4 Carefully spoon the batter evenly into the friand moulds. Place 5 blueberries on top of each friand and sprinkle with almonds.

5 Bake for 20 minutes until firm to the touch, risen and golden. Leave to cool in the tin for 5 minutes before carefully turning out onto a wire rack to cool completely. Serve fresh and just warm.

Best eaten fresh on the day they are made.

VARIATION
LEMON & GINGER FRIANDS – omit the blueberries, orange zest and flaked almonds. Peel and grate a 2cm (¾ inch) piece of ginger and add to the friand mixture with the zest of 1 lemon and 1 tablespoon poppy seeds. Drizzle with Lemon Syrup (see page 198) and top with 40g (1½oz) chopped stem ginger.

LEFT Orange and blueberry friands baked in their distinctive tin.
RIGHT Lemon, poppy seed and ginger friands with a delicate lemon syrup.

I have enjoyed making these raspberry jam buns for as long as I have been baking. Comparatively low in butter compared with other bakes, they are flavoured with currants and nutmeg. The secret is to shape the bun to create the largest well that will hold the biggest dollop of jam or raspberry fruit spread. Healthier than a doughnut but with just as much fun trying to save the jam mouthful to last! They are a great introductory bake or to make with children.

MAKES 9 BUNS

Raspberry Jam Buns

250g (9oz) self-raising flour

100g (3½oz) wholemeal flour

1 heaped teaspoon ground nutmeg

1 teaspoon baking powder

125g (4½oz) unsalted butter

125g (4½oz) soft light brown sugar

75g (2¾oz) currants, soaked in 4 tablespoons boiling water for 1 hour

1 large egg, beaten

3 tablespoons milk

½ a jar seedless raspberry jam

1 Preheat the oven to 180°C/gas 4. Line a baking tray with non-stick baking parchment.

2 Sift together the flours, nutmeg and baking powder. Rub the butter into the flour until it resembles fine breadcrumbs, then stir in the sugar and currants. Make a well in the centre and add the egg and enough milk to make a stiff but not dry dough.

3 Shape the dough into 9 balls and place apart on the baking tray. Press a wooden spoon handle into the bun and give it a little wiggle to make a well.

4 Stir the jam until smooth, then place a large teaspoon of jam into the well of each bun.

5 Bake for 20 minutes until golden brown. Leave to cool for a minute before lifting each bun on to a wire rack to cool.

Store for up to 7 days in an airtight container in a cool, dry place. Not suitable for freezing.

3

4

Chocolate-dusted Orange Madeleines

MAKES 18 MADELEINES

2 eggs

100g (3½oz) golden caster sugar

100g (3½oz) melted butter, plus
  extra for greasing

3 tablespoons drinking chocolate,
  plus extra for dusting

75g (2¾oz) plain flour

25g (1oz) ground almonds

grated zest of 1 orange

¾ teaspoon baking powder

The French madeleine is a delicate genoise sponge baked in a distinctive shell mould and is often made with lemon or orange zest and ground almonds. They are the perfect size to be satisfying with a cup of tea or coffee. They need no additional embellishment and should be enjoyed as fresh to baking as possible.

1 Whisk the eggs and sugar together in a large bowl until frothy. Fold in the remaining ingredients, then leave to stand for about 20 minutes to thicken.

2 Preheat the oven to 200°C/gas 6. Butter a 12-hole madeleine tray and dust with drinking chocolate.

3 Transfer to a jug or large piping bag and carefully fill each mould until three-quarters full (you will need to bake in batches to use all the batter). Bake for 8–10 minutes until golden and risen in the middle. Leave to cool for 5 minutes before lifting each madeleine out to cool on a wire rack.

Best eaten fresh on the day they are made.

VARIATION
Replace the orange zest with lemon zest or vanilla bean paste.

2

3

Scones are so versatile as they can be enjoyed as a sweet or savoury treat. Go back to basics with plain buttermilk scones, add a favourite fruit with berry or lemon and sultana scones or go savoury with pumpkin scones.

Scones are traditionally served for Afternoon Tea with lashings of clotted cream and strawberry jam. They are a satisfying bake enjoyed with a little butter with morning coffee or an afternoon cup of tea. They can be easily embellished with spices such as cinnamon, lemon and ginger, apple and brown sugar or chocolate and delicious both savoury and sweet. I often make scones for lunches with salads or soups instead of bread.

TOP TIP

Stamp out the scones – do not twist them as this will cause the scones to rise unevenly.

Plain Buttermilk Scones

MAKES 6 SCONES

225g (8oz) self-raising flour, plus
    extra for dusting

½ teaspoon salt

55g (1¾oz) unsalted butter

30g (1¼oz) golden caster sugar

150ml (5fl oz) buttermilk

1 egg, beaten, or milk, to glaze

1 Preheat the oven to 220°C/gas 7. Flour a baking sheet.

2 Sift the flour with the salt in a large bowl. Rub in the butter until the mixture resembles breadcrumbs, then stir in the sugar. Make a deep well in the flour and pour in the buttermilk. Mix to form a soft dough with a knife – do not overwork.

3 Transfer the dough to a lightly floured surface and knead very gently to bring the dough together. Lightly roll or press the dough to a thickness of 2.5cm (1 inch) and stamp out 6 rounds with a 6cm (2¼ inch) pastry cutter.

4 Place the rounds on the floured baking sheet and brush with a beaten egg or milk to glaze. Bake for 8–10 minutes or until well risen and brown. Leave to cool on a wire rack and serve warm with clotted cream and strawberry jam.

Best eaten fresh on the day they are made.

VARIATIONS

BERRY SCONES – make the base mixture as above. Roll the dough to two 15 x 25cm (6 x 10 inch) rectangles. Spread some Berry Compote (see page 19) over one rectangle and place the other rectangle on top. Cut into triangles and place on a baking sheet lined with non-stick baking parchment. Brush with milk and sprinkle with demerara sugar. Bake for 20 minutes until golden brown.

LEMON & SULTANA SCONES – make as above, but add the grated zest of 1 lemon and 30g (1¼oz) sultanas. Serve with homemade Lemon Curd (see page 18).

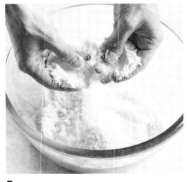

2

3

4

Pumpkin Scones

MAKES 6 SCONES

225g (8oz) self-raising flour, plus extra for dusting

1 teaspoon baking powder

40g (1½oz) unsalted butter

60g (2¼oz) grated Cheddar

1 tablespoon finely chopped rosemary

200g (7oz) canned pumpkin purée

80ml (3fl oz) milk, plus extra to glaze

1 Preheat the oven to 220°C/gas 7. Flour a baking sheet.

2 Sift the flour with the baking powder in a large bowl. Rub in the butter until the mixture resembles breadcrumbs, then stir in the cheese and rosemary.

3 Make a deep well in the flour and add the pumpkin purée and just enough milk to make a soft dough with a knife – do not overwork.

4 Tip the dough out onto a lightly floured surface and knead very gently to bring the dough together.

5 Lightly roll or press the dough to a thickness of 2.5cm (1 inch) and stamp out 6 rounds with a 6cm (2¼ inch) pastry cutter.

6 Place on the floured baking sheet and brush with milk to glaze. Bake for 8–10 minutes or until well risen and brown. Leave to cool on a wire rack and serve warm with butter.

Best eaten fresh on the day they are made.

Biscuits & Cookies

Cookies are the perfect accompaniment at any time of the day – and how lovely to bake your own so you can pack them full of flavour and texture and not just sugar, fat and salt. These recipes use ingredients with integrity to tickle your taste buds, satisfy your palate and show off your baking skills. From super simple nut butter jam biscuits through to honey nut nougat I am sure you will find delicious, nutritious recipes here that will become firm favourites for successful baking.

Anzac Biscuits

These rustic biscuits made with rolled oats are egg free and were originally made by the soldiers' wives to send abroad without spoiling. Oats are a valuable source of thiamine (Vitamin B1), iron and fibre. They contain antioxidants, which can help prevent heart disease and contain beta-glucan slow-release complex carbohydrate, which may help those with Type-2 diabetes control their blood sugar levels. They are quick and easy to make and a perfect breakfast on the go for all those who enjoy porridge.

F EF

MAKES 18–22 BISCUITS

85g (3oz) rolled oats

40g (1½oz) pinhead oatmeal

85g (3oz) desiccated coconut

100g (3½oz) plain flour

100g (3½oz) soft light brown sugar

1 teaspoon ground cinnamon

100g (3½oz) unsalted butter

1 tablespoon golden syrup

1 teaspoon bicarbonate of soda

1 Preheat the oven to 180°C/gas 4. Line a baking tray with non-stick baking parchment.

2 Place the oats, pinhead oatmeal, coconut, flour, sugar and cinnamon in a bowl and stir.

3 Melt the butter and golden syrup together in a small pan. Blend the bicarbonate of soda with 2 tablespoons boiling water and add it to the butter and syrup.

4 Make a well in the dry ingredients and pour in the buttery syrup. Stir until everything is fully incorporated.

5 Place a spoonful of the mixture (each weighing about 20g/¾oz) onto the baking sheet, spaced well apart, and bake for 8–10 minutes until golden. These biscuits will spread.

6 Remove from the oven, leave to cool for 1 minute, then transfer to a wire rack with a palette knife to cool completely.

Store for up to 21 days in an airtight container at room temperature. Not suitable for freezing.

TOP TIP

Pinhead oatmeal is the inner kernel of the whole oats, which have been roughly chopped, offering a chewier, nutty flavoured oat with added texture.

Nut Butter Jam Biscuits

These morsels are packed full of energy, and as they are homemade, contain no refined sugar and no added salt. You can make them small enough to be a satisfying bite and therefore portion and calorie controlled! They are fun to make with children and great for beginners or those with little time.

MAKES 36 BISCUITS

150g (5½oz) unsalted butter

150g (5½oz) soft light brown sugar

2 egg yolks

100g (3½oz) peanut butter (crunchy, no added salt) – or cashew, almond or hazelnut butter

200g (7oz) self-raising flour, plus extra for dusting

200g (7oz) strawberry jam

1 Preheat the oven to 180°C/gas 4. Line a baking sheet with non-stick baking parchment.

2 Cream the butter and sugar together in a bowl until softened. Add the egg yolks and peanut butter and blend until well mixed. Add the flour and stir to make a soft dough.

3 With lightly floured hands, break off walnut-sized pieces of dough (each weighing about 20g/¾oz). Place them on the prepared baking sheet, spaced well apart, and press gently to flatten them slightly.

4 Make a deep well in the centre of each flattened ball of dough using the handle of a wooden spoon or your thumb; the cookies will flatten and spread out as they bake.

5 Stir the jam until it is smooth and a little runny, then spoon a teaspoonful into the centre of each cookie. Bake in the centre of the oven for 10–12 minutes until golden. Transfer to a wire rack to cool.

Store for up to 5 days in an airtight container at room temperature. Not suitable for freezing.

TOP TIPS

Nut Butters and Jams:
- Look for nut butters with no added salt, sugar or oil.
- Store in a cool dry place to avoid rancidity.
- Look for jams with raw sugar where possible.

Chocolate chunk cookies are a staple in many homes – so how can these be made healthier? I have included a higher cocoa solids chocolate, which will reduce the sweetness, but still deliver a real chocolate hit. I have then used hazelnut butter and chopped roasted hazelnuts to add flavour and texture, reducing the overall amount of butter and have only used an unrefined light brown sugar to create a chewy cookie. I have also made them slightly smaller – a portion-controlled cookie!

Chocolate Chunk Cookies

MAKES 12 COOKIES

300g (10½oz) dark chocolate (between 55% and 70% cocoa solids)

85g (3oz) unsalted butter

100g (3½oz) light muscovado sugar

100g (3½oz) hazelnut butter (crunchy)

1 medium egg

1 teaspoon vanilla extract

100g (3½oz) self-raising flour

100g (3½oz) roughly chopped roasted hazelnuts

1 Preheat the oven to 180°C/gas 4. Line a baking sheet with non-stick baking parchment.

2 Chop 200g (7oz) of the chocolate into rough chunks. Melt the remaining chocolate in a large heatproof bowl over a pan of simmering water or in the microwave. Leave to cool slightly.

3 Stir in the butter, sugar, hazelnut butter, egg and vanilla and beat until smooth. Stir in the flour, chopped hazelnuts and remaining chocolate chunks. Cover and chill the mixture for 10 minutes.

4 Drop 12 spoonfuls of the mixture onto the prepared baking sheet with plenty of room between each spoonful to allow for spreading.

5 Bake for 10 minutes until very lightly browned. Be careful not to overbake, they should be gently chewy on the inside. Remove from the oven and leave to cool for 3 minutes before lifting them on to a wire rack with a palette knife to cool completely. Enjoy fresh on the day while still warm!

Store for up to 3 days in an airtight container at room temperature. Not suitable for freezing.

VARIATION
Substitute the hazelnut butter and hazelnuts with almonds, cashews or peanuts to find your favourite flavour.

Vanilla and Chocolate
Party Rings decorated
with dark chocolate
and coloured sprinkles.

Party Rings

MAKES 16–18 BISCUITS

250g (9oz) unsalted butter, softened

75g (2¾oz) golden icing sugar

250g (9oz) plain flour

50g (1¾oz) cornflour

60g (2¼oz) ground almonds

2 teaspoons vanilla bean paste

50g (1¾oz) dark chocolate, melted

sprinkles, to decorate

These soft creamed biscuits are egg free and hand piped. They have a short, slightly crumbly texture and literally melt in the mouth thanks to the inclusion of icing sugar and cornflour. The ground almonds add moisture from the natural oils, along with great flavour and texture.

1 Preheat the oven to 180°C/gas 4. Line a baking sheet with non-stick baking parchment.

2 Place all the ingredients, except the chocolate, in a food processor or blender and beat on a medium-high speed until well combined and smooth.

3 Fill a large piping bag with an open star nozzle and the biscuit batter. Pipe fingers, rounds or S-shaped biscuits on the prepared baking sheets.

4 Bake for 12–15 minutes until very lightly browned. Remove from the oven and leave to cool for 3 minutes before lifting them onto a wire rack with a palette knife to cool completely.

5 Melt the chocolate in a bowl and fill a piping bag. Snip the end and drizzle chocolate over the biscuits. Decorate with the sprinkles, then leave to set.

Store for up to 3 days in an airtight container at room temperature. Not suitable for freezing.

VARIATION
CHOCOLATE PARTY RINGS – replace 70g (2¾oz) of the plain flour with cocoa powder.

These ginger biscuits are classic treacle biscuits made with unrefined sugar, butter, flour and spices, and with no added salt. They are simple to make but with such a distinctive flavour and texture they are instantly satisfying and portion controlled.

Chewy Ginger Biscuits

MAKES 16 BISCUITS

85g (3oz) unsalted butter

100g (3½oz) soft light brown sugar

1 medium egg

2 tablespoons black treacle

125g (4½oz) plain flour

1 teaspoon ground ginger

1 teaspoon ground cinnamon

¼ teaspoon ground cloves

1 teaspoon bicarbonate of soda

FOR THE LEMON GLACÉ ICING

50g (1¾oz) icing sugar

juice of 1 lemon

1 Preheat the oven to 190°C/gas 5. Line a baking sheet with non-stick baking parchment.

2 Place the butter in a pan to melt, then leave to cool slightly. Add the sugar, egg and black treacle and beat until smooth.

3 In a separate bowl, sift together the dry ingredients. Beat the dry ingredients into the sugar and butter mixture and stir to a dough. Wrap the dough in cling film and chill for 2 hours.

4 Pinch off walnut-sized pieces of the dough (each weighing about 20g/¾oz) and roll them into balls. Place on the prepared baking sheet about 5cm (2 inches) apart. Bake for 8–10 minutes until they're browned, spread out and dry on the surface. Transfer to a wire rack to cool.

5 Make the lemon glacé icing by mixing the icing sugar with enough lemon juice to make a thin runny icing. Fill a piping bag and snip the end. Drizzle the icing over the biscuits while they are on the rack. Leave to set for 30 minutes before serving.

Store for up to 3 days in an airtight container at room temperature. Not suitable for freezing.

These are the English style macaroons rather than the little French sandwiched delicacies. Larger round almond biscuits, they are traditionally baked on rice paper circles. They are by nature gluten free and dairy free, made with ground almonds and golden caster sugar. Adjust the size to make small petits four-style biscuits and enjoy these instead of chocolates. These macaroons are fun to make and package in bags or boxes as gifts.

Almond Macaroons

 GF DF LF

MAKES 16–18 MACAROONS

2 medium egg whites

125g (4½oz) ground almonds

175g (6oz) golden caster sugar

16–18 blanched almond halves

TOP TIP

Bake the macaroons on discs of edible rice paper and package in clear bags tied with ribbon.

1 Preheat the oven to 180°C/gas 4. Line a baking sheet with non-stick baking parchment.

2 Whisk the egg whites until foamy. Place the ground almonds in a separate bowl and add one-quarter of the egg whites. Mix, then add half the sugar. Mix again before adding another quarter of the egg whites and the remaining sugar. Add another quarter of the egg and mix. The mixture should now be soft enough to shape into 16–18 walnut-sized balls (each weighing 20g/¾oz). If it is too stiff, add the remaining egg whites.

3 Place the balls on the prepared baking sheet, spaced well apart. Brush each with a little cold water, then press an almond lightly on the top. Bake for 20 minutes until very lightly browned. Be careful not to overbake, they should be gently chewy on the inside. Transfer to a wire rack to cool.

Store for up to 14 days in an airtight container at room temperature. Not suitable for freezing.

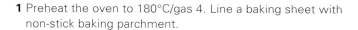

VARIATION
Add 1½ teaspoons freeze-dried raspberry or blackcurrant powder to the ground almonds to flavour the macaroons.

Homemade nougat is deceptively
easy to make, dairy free and packed
full of roasted nuts and fruits.

Nougat is a dairy-free, gluten-free, honey meringue packed full of roasted nuts and semi-dried fruits, rolled in a thin slab and cut into bite-sized treats. It is important to reach the desired temperatures to ensure the eggs are safe to eat and the nougat sets firm but not too brittle and hard. Your choice of honey will subtly affect the flavour as too will your choice of nuts and fruits.

Nougat

GF DF LF

MAKES 48 BITE-SIZED PIECES

420g (15oz) golden caster sugar

100g (3½oz) liquid glucose

75ml (2½fl oz) water

125g (4½oz) orange blossom honey

2 large egg whites

125g (4½oz) flaked almonds, roasted (see page 94)

125g (4½oz) roasted whole hazelnuts

75g (2¾oz) roasted pistachios

75g (2¾oz) naturally coloured glacé cherries or dried cherries

75g (2¾oz) chopped apricots

2 x A3 (or 4 x A4) sheets of rice paper

" TOP TIP
Crystallized ginger and figs are great alternative ingredients. Also, experiment with different kinds of honey to find your favourite.

1 Place 400g (14oz) of the sugar in a saucepan with the glucose and just enough water to cover. Melt over a medium heat and continue until the temperature reaches 135°C (275°F) on a thermometer. Add the honey and continue to heat to 145°C (293°F).

2 Meanwhile, place the egg whites and the remaining sugar in a clean bowl and whisk to the stiff peak stage. With the whisk on medium speed, pour the hot syrup carefully and steadily into the meringue.

3 Once all the syrup has been poured in, continue to whisk on full speed for 5 minutes until the meringue has cooled, thickened and is glossy and lukewarm to touch. Carefully fold the nuts and fruits into the meringue.

4 Lay one sheet of rice paper on a baking sheet and spread the nougat evenly onto the paper. Place the other sheet on top and use a rolling pin to achieve an even finish. (If you are using A4 sheets, make 2 smaller batches.) Leave to set overnight to cool and firm up.

5 Use a large knife to cut the nougat into bite-sized pieces.

Store for up to 14 days in an airtight container at room temperature. Not suitable for home freezing.

1

2

3

3

4

TOP Almond and Cranberry Biscotti.
BOTTOM Chocolate and Pistachio Biscotti
– dairy-free intensely crunchy biscuits.

Biscotti are also known as 'cantuccini' and are Italian almond biscuits that originated in the city of Prato. They are twice-baked, oblong-shaped, dry and crunchy. Traditionally, they are dipped in vin santo but growing in popularity and are often served with coffee and tea. Biscotti are composed exclusively of flour, sugar, eggs and nuts including pine nuts, hazelnuts or almonds that are not roasted or skinned. The traditional recipe uses no form of yeast or fat – so these biscuits are low in calories and dairy free. The biscuit dough is cooked twice with the second baking defining how hard the biscotti will be.

Almond & Cranberry Biscotti

MAKES 36–40 BISCOTTI

250g (9oz) plain flour, plus extra for dusting

200g (7oz) golden caster sugar

2 teaspoons baking powder

2 large eggs

150g (5½oz) dried cranberries

150g (5½oz) whole almonds

grated zest of 1 orange (or 3 drops of orange oil)

golden icing sugar, for dusting

1 Preheat the oven to 190°C/gas 5. Line a baking tray with non-stick baking parchment.

2 Mix the flour, sugar and baking powder in a bowl. Add the eggs and whisk until the mix resembles a crumble topping. Add the cranberries, almonds and orange and stir to form a soft dough, taking care not to overmix at this stage. The dough should be gently crumbly but not tough.

3 Turn the dough out onto a lightly floured surface and divide it into three. Carefully roll each into a log about 3cm (1¼ inches) wide and place them apart on the prepared baking tray. Bake for 20 minutes until they are lightly browned and firm to the touch.

4 Remove the baking tray from the oven and turn the oven down to 50°C/lowest possible gas setting. Leave the logs to cool on the baking sheet, dusting them with golden icing sugar while they are still warm.

5 Place the cooled logs on a board and cut them on an angle into about 2cm (¾ inch) thick slices. Place the biscotti on baking sheets, allowing space between each one for the air to circulate, and bake for 1 hour until they have dried out and are slightly brittle.

Store for up to 7 days in an airtight container at room temperature. Not suitable for freezing.

These biscotti combine chocolate and pistachios, which you can happily dunk into your morning cappuccino offering a dairy free, lower fat, reduced calorie, deliciously crunchy biscuit bite. You're welcome!

Chocolate & Pistachio Biscotti

MAKES 20–24 BISCOTTI

1 large egg

110g (4oz) golden caster sugar

110g (4oz) plain flour

2 tablespoons cocoa powder

150g (5½oz) pistachios, shelled

100g (3½oz) dairy-free dark chocolate chips (70% cocoa solids) – or a bar of dairy-free chocolate, grated

1 Preheat the oven to 190°C/gas 5. Line a baking tray with non-stick baking parchment.

2 Whisk the egg and sugar in a large bowl until the texture is light and fluffy.

3 Stir in the plain flour and cocoa powder and then add the pistachio and chocolate chips. The dough should be quite sticky at this stage. Flour your hands and divide the dough into 2 portions

4 Shape each portion into a log about 3cm (1¼ inches) wide and place on the prepared baking sheet. Bake in the oven for about 20 minutes until firm to the touch with a good crust.

5 Remove the baking tray from the oven, transfer to a wire rack and allow to cool. Reduce the oven temperature to 50°C/lowest possible gas setting.

6 Using a sharp serrated knife, cut slices about 2cm (¾ inch) wide, then place the pieces back on the baking tray, allowing space between each one for the air to circulate. Bake for 1 hour until they have dried out and are slightly brittle.

Store for up to 7 days in an airtight container at room temperature. Not suitable for freezing.

4

6

6

Homemade decorated biscuits are a wonderful gift and are fun to make. I have used white royal icing for an authentic decoration. This biscuit dough can be used to create cookies throughout the year from baby showers to birthdays, Halloween to Thanksgiving. For added sparkle, finish the cookies with an edible pearl lustre spray.

Snowflake Vanilla Biscuits

ICING TOP TIPS

- Look for cartons of lightly pasteurized egg whites available in the chilled section of the supermarket. These are safe, have up to 1 month's shelf life unopened and a 7 day shelf life once opened if kept refrigerated. The cartons can also be frozen and defrosted for use as required.
- The added lemon juice strengthens the icing and imparts a subtle flavour.
- Once you have made the royal icing, if it looks grainy or really stiff, add a little more egg white and continue to whisk for 2 minutes on high speed.
- Royal icing once made will keep in an airtight container for up to 7 days. Re-whisk daily before use.

TOP TIP

Use a straw to make a small hole in the cookie before you bake them so that you can hang them from a ribbon.

Snowflake Vanilla Biscuits

**MAKES 24–30 COOKIES
DEPENDING ON THE SIZE**

200g (7oz) unsalted butter,
　softened

200g (7oz) unrefined caster sugar

1 medium egg, beaten

400g (14oz) plain flour, plus extra
　for dusting

1 teaspoon baking powder

1 teaspoon vanilla powder or
　2 teaspoons vanilla bean paste

FOR THE ROYAL ICING

140g (5oz) egg whites (fresh or
　lightly pasteurized), at room
　temperature

600–750g (1lb 5oz–1lb 10oz) white
　or golden icing sugar

juice of 1 lemon

1 Cream the butter and sugar together, then add the beaten egg and mix to combine. Gently fold in the flour, baking powder and vanilla powder and mix until a dough forms. Wrap the dough in cling film and chill for 30 minutes.

2 Preheat the oven to 180°C/gas 4. Line a baking sheet with non-stick baking parchment. Lightly flour a work surface and roll the dough to a thickness of 0.75cm (¼–½ inch). Stamp out snowflake cookie shapes and place on the prepared baking sheet, spaced well apart. Bake for 10–12 minutes until pale golden, then transfer to a wire rack to cool.

3 To make the icing, whisk the egg whites in a bowl until they're soft and foamy. Add the icing sugar. Whisk on super slow speed until the sugar is incorporated, then on high speed until the icing is mallow, glossy and has the consistency of freshly whipped double cream. Pass the lemon juice through a tea strainer into the bowl and continue to whisk for 2 minutes. The icing should be glossy and thick but not overstiff or dry.

4 To decorate, fill piping bags with plain or star nozzles and the icing. Hand pipe the cookies to decorate. Alternatively, use ready-made tubes of coloured icings and gels.

Store for up to 28 days in an airtight container at room temperature. Not suitable for freezing.

4

Gingerbread cookies are wonderful to decorate for the holidays. As simple or as intricate as you like – you don't need to invest in a huge amount of money, time and skill to achieve a fabulous result that will build your confidence in sugar decoration. These spiced cookies are perfect for Halloween, Thanksgiving and Christmas. Use your own cookie cutters to create decorations, gifts or birthday treats instead of the wreath.

Gingerbread Wreath

**MAKES 24–30 COOKIES
DEPENDING ON THE SIZE**

425g (15oz) plain flour, plus extra
  for dusting

1 tablespoon ground ginger

2 teaspoons ground cinnamon

½ teaspoon ground nutmeg

¼ teaspoon ground cloves

1 level teaspoon baking powder

½ teaspoon bicarbonate of soda

1 teaspoon vanilla powder (or
  2 teaspoons vanilla extract)

140g (5oz) unsalted butter,
  softened

165g (5¾oz) muscovado (dark
  brown) sugar

1 large egg yolk

165g (5¾oz) black treacle

1–2 tablespoons milk

TO DECORATE

1 quantity of Royal Icing (see
  page 86)

green and red food colouring gels

red sugar candy pearls

1 Preheat the oven to 180°C/gas 4. Line a baking sheet with non-stick baking parchment.

2 In a mixing bowl, sift together the flour, spices and raising agents – add the vanilla powder here, if using.

3 Cream the butter and sugar together in a bowl. Blend the egg yolk together with the black treacle and milk. Add the vanilla extract here, if using. Whisk into the creamed mixture. Add the flour to the batter and mix until the dough just comes together. Wrap the dough in cling film and chill for 30 minutes.

4 Lightly knead the dough and roll out on a lightly floured work surface. Use a 15cm (6 inch) and 25cm (10 inch) round tin to cut out a ring of dough for the base of the wreath from the rolled out dough, then carefully place it on the prepared sheet.

5 Use a 5.5cm (2¼ inch) and 8.5cm (3¼ inch) holly cookie cutter to cut out 36 holly cookies and place them on the prepared baking sheets (or bake in batches if necessary).

6 Draw a bow on card (or use a bow cookie cutter), cut out and use as a template to make the bow. Bake the holly cookies for 8 minutes, the bow for 10 minutes and the wreath for 12–15 minutes until firm and golden. Leave to cool on the tray, then transfer to a wire rack.

7 Separate the royal icing into 4 bowls and colour 2 shades of green, a red and leave one white. To ice the wreath, fill 2 piping bags with a no. 2 nozzle and 1 tablespoon of the green icing in separate bags. Pipe outlines on the holly cookies. Thin the remaining green icing with water to flooding consistency and spoon into a piping bag. Snip the end and flood the cookies, using a paintbrush to push the icing up to the piped line. Leave to set for 1 hour, then pipe over the icing to create texture and design.

Continued overleaf...

TOP TIP

Bake your favourite cookies and decorate with ready-made icing and sprinkles.

8 For the bow, pipe the outline in red with a no. 2 nozzle and flood with thinned red icing. Fill a piping bag with no. 3 nozzle and slightly thinned white icing. Pipe polka dots on the red icing while it is still wet, then leave all the iced components to set overnight.

9 To assemble, start by fixing the bow in position on the wreath base with stiff white royal icing. Fix the holly pieces in place using white royal icing to secure them. Finish with red sugar candy pearls iced into position with white royal icing. Leave to set for 2 hours.

Store for up to 28 days in an airtight container at room temperature. Not suitable for freezing.

7

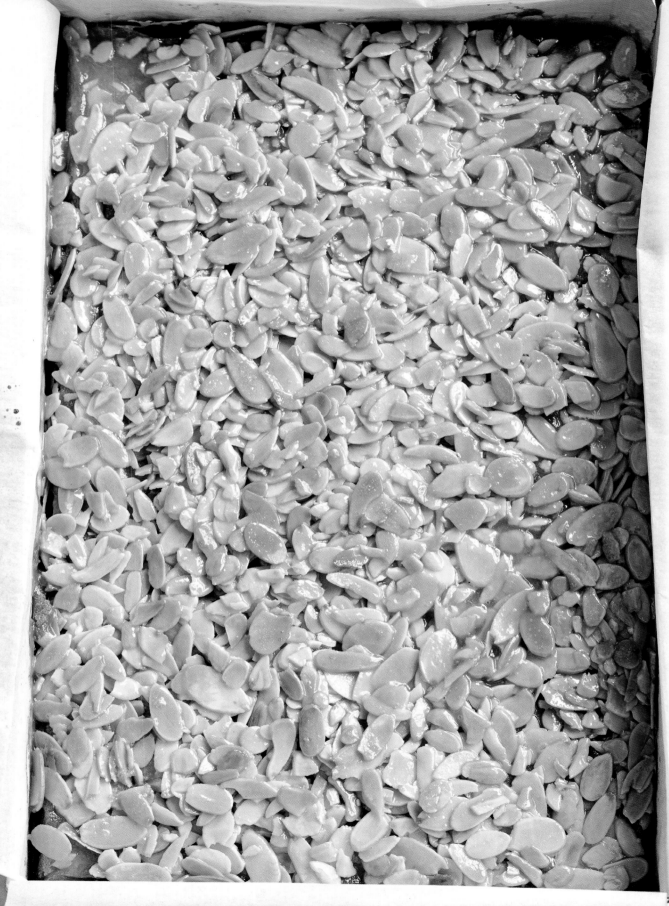

Bars & Flapjacks

Traybakes or bars are quick and easy to make and bake and can be a staple in most homes for packed lunches, morning coffee or afternoon snack time. I have adjusted these recipes so they can all be baked in the same size tin – offering you the flexibility to choose a different recipe each week. From simple flapjacks and shortbreads to layered bakes and brownies, these bars will build your confidence in baking and build your repertoire of delicious bakes.

MAKES 16 BARS

225g (8oz) unsalted butter
    (or vegan margarine or spread
    for a dairy-free alternative)

120g (4½oz) clear honey

100g (3½oz) soft light brown sugar

350g (12oz) rolled oats

50g (1¾oz) flaked almonds

70g (2½oz) sultanas

70g (2½oz) dried apricots, chopped

80g (3oz) prunes, chopped

100g (3½oz) dates, chopped

2 teaspoons fennel seeds

2 teaspoons chia seeds

2 tablespoons pumpkin seeds

2 tablespoons linseeds

Packed with energy-giving, mineral-rich fruits, seeds, nuts and oats, these little pocket rockets will keep you fuelled all day and satisfy any cravings.

Date, Seed & Honey Power Bars

1 Preheat the oven to 160°C/ gas 3. Line the base and sides of a 30 x 20cm (12 x 8 inch) tin with non-stick baking parchment.

2 Melt the butter and honey together. Toss all the dry ingredients together, then pour over the melted butter and honey. Stir to combine.

3 Transfer to the prepared tin, press down and bake for 40 minutes until golden. Leave to cool, then chill well before cutting into 16 bars.

Store for up to 7 days in an airtight container in the refrigerator. Not suitable for freezing.

Iron Bars

MAKES 16 BARS

225g (8oz) unsalted butter
    (or vegan margarine or spread
    for a dairy-free alternative)

120g (4½oz) clear honey

100g (3½oz) soft light brown
    sugar

350g (12oz) rolled oats

75g (2¾oz) cashews, roughly
    chopped

75g (2¾oz) sunflower seeds

200g (7oz) chopped organic
    ready-to-eat apricots

A healthy boost of iron will improve the condition of your skin, hair and nails as well as providing energy, warmth and vitality. Apricots, cashews and sunflower seeds are naturally rich sources of iron – enjoy these iron-rich bars with a glass of orange juice, high in vitamin C for maximum absorption.

1 Preheat the oven to 150°C/gas 2. Line the base and sides of a 30 x 20cm (12 x 8 inch) tin with non-stick baking parchment. Melt the butter and honey together. Toss all the dry ingredients together, then pour over the melted butter and honey. Stir to combine.

2 Transfer to the prepared tin, press down and bake for 40 minutes until golden. Leave to cool, then chill well before cutting into 16 bars.

Store for up to 7 days in an airtight container in the refrigerator. Not suitable for freezing.

These squares are deliciously nutty and satisfyingly sweet.
I like to serve them as an alternative to pudding, with coffee
after a meal. They deliver such a hit of flavour, crunch and
sweetness, one small square is the perfect controlled portion.

Almond Toscaner

MAKES 24 SQUARES

100g (3½oz) unsalted butter, room
    temperature

190g (6¾oz) golden caster sugar

190g (6¾oz) ground almonds

240g (8½oz) whole eggs (about
    4 large eggs)

50g (1¾oz) plain flour

1 teaspoon almond extract

FOR THE TOPPING

100g (3½oz) unsalted butter

100g (3½oz) golden caster sugar

100g (3½oz) liquid glucose

50ml (2fl oz) milk

150g (5½oz) flaked almonds,
    roasted (see Tip below)

1 Preheat the oven to 190°C/gas 5. Line the base and sides of a
30 x 20cm (12 x 8 inch) tin with non-stick baking parchment.
Beat together the butter, sugar and almonds in a bowl, add the
eggs slowly, then fold in the flour. Transfer to the prepared tin and
bake for about 16–18 minutes.

2 Meanwhile, make the topping. Put the butter, sugar, glucose and
milk in a pan, bring to the boil, then simmer for 1–2 minutes,
stirring. Remove from the heat and stir in the roasted almonds.

3 Once the base has baked, remove the toscaner from the oven and
turn the oven temperature up to 200°C/gas 6. Spread the topping
over the sponge, return to the oven and bake for 6–8 minutes until
golden. Leave to cool completely in the tin, then cut into 24 squares.

Store for 2–3 days in an airtight container at room temperature. Best
eaten on the day they are made – the topping will soften and become
more chewy with keeping, but this does not deter from the flavour!

VARIATION

*Add the grated zest of 1 orange to the almond
base before baking, and 1 tablespoon (50g/1¾oz)
apricot conserve to the topping.*

" TOP TIP

To roast nuts: preheat
the oven to 150°C/gas 2.
Spread the nuts out on a
baking tray and bake for
15 minutes until just
turning golden.

5

Chocolate and coconut have a wonderful affinity and these bars combine the best of both ingredients – with a chocolate coconut shortbread topped with an intense, rich dark chocolate ganache. I have used raw sugar and wholemeal flour for added nutrition.

Chocolate Coconut Shortbread

MAKES 16 SQUARES

300g (10½oz) unsalted butter, melted

40g (1½oz) cocoa powder

300g (10½oz) wholemeal flour

210g (7½oz) soft light brown sugar

3 teaspoons baking powder

150g (5½oz) desiccated coconut

FOR THE CHOCOLATE GANACHE

175ml (6fl oz) double cream

150g (5½oz) dark chocolate (between 55 and 70% cocoa solids), broken into pieces

1 Preheat the oven 190°C/gas 5. Line the base and sides of a 30 x 20cm (12 x 8 inch) tin with non-stick baking parchment.

2 Melt the butter in a large saucepan and stir in the cocoa. Remove from the heat and stir in all the remaining ingredients. Transfer to the prepared tin and press down. Bake for 25–30 minutes until risen, firm and coming away from the sides of the tin.

3 Remove from the oven, transfer to a wire rack and leave to cool in the tin for 5 minutes.

4 To make the ganache, bring the cream to the boil in a saucepan, remove from the heat and stir in the broken chocolate. Stir until melted and smooth.

5 Top the shortbread with the chocolate ganache, leave to set, then cut into 16 squares.

Store for up to 7 days in an airtight container at room temperature or chilled. Not suitable for freezing.

Date & Apple Squares

 F   EF

MAKES 16 SQUARES

350g (12oz) cooking apples,
    peeled, cored and chopped

grated zest and juice of 1 lemon

2 teaspoons ground cinnamon

350g (12oz) Medjool dates, stoned

140g (5oz) soft light brown sugar

300g (10½oz) plain flour

200g (7oz) rolled porridge oats

250g (9oz) unsalted butter, melted

These bars are nutritious with oats, apple and dates that are rich in complex carbohydrates, vitamins, minerals and fibre. The bars are naturally sweet, so I have reduced the overall sugar in this delicious oaty flapjack.

1 Preheat the oven to 180°C/gas 4. Line the base and sides of a 30 x 20cm (12 x 8 inch) tin with non-stick baking parchment.

2 Place the apple in a saucepan with the lemon zest and juice and the cinnamon. Bring to the boil and simmer over a low heat for 5 minutes until tender.

3 Add the dates and 40g (1½oz) of the sugar and cook for a further 5 minutes until the mixture is a stiff paste, but not dry. Be careful not to let the mixture boil dry. Add 2–3 tablespoons water if this is looking likely. Remove from the heat.

4 Put the flour, remaining sugar and oats into a bowl and mix together. Make a well in the centre and pour in the melted butter. Mix together to form an oaty, crumbly mixture.

5 Press half the oat mixture into the base of the tin and press down firmly. Spread the apple and date mixture over the oaty base, then top with the remaining oat mixture. Press down firmly.

6 Bake for 35 minutes until golden. Leave to cool in the tin, then cut into 16 squares.

Store for up to 5 days in an airtight container at room temperature or chilled. Not suitable for freezing.

MAKES 16 SQUARES

175g (6oz) unsalted butter

175g (6oz) golden caster sugar

150g (5½oz) self-raising flour

1 teaspoon baking powder

100g (3½oz) ground almonds

3 large eggs

2 teaspoons vanilla extract

150g (5½oz) soured cream

FOR THE CRUMBLE TOPPING

25g (1oz) unsalted butter, melted

50g (1¾oz) plain flour, sifted

35g (1¼oz) golden caster sugar

15g (½oz) hazelnuts, chopped

15g (½oz) rolled oats

1 tablespoon honey

½ teaspoon ground ginger

FOR THE RHUBARB

400g (14oz) rhubarb (untrimmed weight)

60g (2¼oz) soft light brown sugar

grated zest of 1 orange

Rhubarb has only 21 calories per 100g (3½oz) with no fat and no cholesterol. Rich in glycosides, rhubarb has long been used as a natural laxative to aid elimination. Rhubarb can be 'forced', which is a practice of growing rhubarb in heated greenhouses by candlelight, excluding all other light to produce a brighter red, more tender, sweeter tasting rhubarb than rhubarb grown outdoors. These bars combine rhubarb with vanilla and soured cream in this soft crumble cake.

Rhubarb & Soured Cream Squares

1 Start by making the crumble topping. Rub the butter into the flour and stir in the sugar. Add the chopped hazelnuts, oats, honey and ginger, then set aside.

2 Next, prepare the rhubarb. Preheat the oven to 200°C/gas 6. Wipe the rhubarb stalks clean, trim and discard the ends. Cut the remainder into 2.5cm (1 inch) pieces and lay on a roasting tray. Sprinkle with the sugar and orange zest. Cover with foil and roast for 15 minutes. Uncover and roast for a further 5 minutes, then leave to cool. Drain off all the juices (you can serve them on the side, thickened with a little custard powder or with icing sugar to make an icing to drizzle over the top if liked).

3 Reduce the oven to 170°C/gas 3. Line the base and sides of a 30 x 20cm (12 x 8 inch) tin with non-stick baking parchment.

4 For the cake, cream the butter and sugar together. Mix the flour with the baking powder and add to the creamed mixture. Add the almonds, eggs, vanilla and soured cream and beat to make a batter. Spread the cake batter in the base of the tin, scatter over the rhubarb, then the crumble topping. Bake for 40–45 minutes until golden and a knife inserted comes out clean. Remove from the oven, transfer to a wire rack and leave to cool in the tin for 10 minutes before cutting into 16 squares. Serve with whipped cream, if liked.

Store for 1–2 days in an airtight container in the refrigerator. Not suitable for freezing.

4

LEFT Quick Chocolate
Brownies are moreish
packed with fruit and nuts.
RIGHT Salted Caramel
Pumpkin Brownies – for a
truly indulgent treat.

Quick Chocolate Brownies

MAKES 16 BROWNIES

150g (5½oz) unsalted butter or non-dairy substitute

75g (2¾oz) dark chocolate (70% cocoa solids), broken into pieces

2 teaspoons cocoa powder

150g (5½oz) roasted mixed nuts (hazelnuts, pistachios, peanuts, pecans, cashews, almonds), roughly chopped (see page 94)

50g (1¾oz) mixed dried fruits (cherries, cranberries, sultanas, raisins)

3 large eggs

300g (10½oz) soft light brown sugar

75g (2¾oz) plain flour

1 heaped teaspoon baking powder

These brownies are packed full of dried fruits and roasted nuts to add flavour, texture as well as added vitamins and minerals. These brownies contain no refined sugar and no salt. They are quick and easy to make so perfect to build confidence in baking.

1 Preheat the oven to 170°C/gas 3. Line the base and sides of a 30 x 20cm (12 x 8 inch) tin with non-stick baking parchment.

2 Melt the butter and chocolate together in a heatproof bowl set over a saucepan of simmering water. Remove from the heat and stir in the cocoa. Stir in all the remaining ingredients. Transfer to the prepared tin and press down. Bake for 25–30 minutes until just set.

3 Remove from the oven, transfer to a wire rack and leave to cool in the tin, before cutting into 16 brownies.

Store for up to 7 days in an airtight container at room temperature or chilled. Suitable for freezing.

VARIATION
Replace the nuts and fruit with 200g (7oz) raspberries folded through the batter before baking or add the grated zest of 2 fresh oranges to the brownie batter before baking.

Pumpkin is an excellent source of beta-carotene – which is converted to vitamin A in the body and is a protective antioxidant. These brownies are delicious throughout the year (with or without the optional caramel), but perfect as a Thanksgiving treat with the addition of the salted caramel.

Salted Caramel Pumpkin Brownies

MAKES 15 BROWNIES

1 quantity of Salted Caramel (see page 106) (optional)

225g (8oz) unsalted butter

300g (10½oz) dark chocolate (55% cocoa solids), broken into pieces

150ml (5fl oz) freshly brewed strong coffee

175g (6oz) soft light brown sugar

175g (6oz) golden caster sugar

2 teaspoons vanilla extract

4 large eggs

150g (5½oz) plain flour

FOR THE PUMPKIN FILLING

115g (4oz) cream cheese, room temperature

115g (4oz) canned pumpkin purée

1 egg

60g (2¼oz) golden caster sugar

1 teaspoon ground cinnamon

½ teaspoon ground ginger

40g (1½oz) plain flour

1 Preheat the oven to 170°C/gas 3. Line the base and sides of a 30 x 20cm (12 x 8 inch) tin with non-stick baking parchment.

2 If using, make the Salted Caramel sauce following the instructions on page 106 and spoon the caramel into a piping bag.

3 Now, make the pumpkin filling. Beat the cream cheese until smooth. Add the pumpkin purée and egg and continue mixing until smooth. Add the sugar, cinnamon, ginger and flour and mix until well combined and smooth. Set aside.

4 Finally, make the brownie batter. Melt together the butter and chocolate in a heatproof bowl (either in a microwave or over a pan of simmering water). Stir in the coffee and leave to cool slightly. Stir in the sugars and vanilla and whisk in the eggs. Finally, fold in the flour until well combined and smooth.

5 Pour half the brownie batter into the prepared tin. Spoon two-thirds of the pumpkin mixture over the brownie batter. Pipe half of the Salted Caramel, if using, over the pumpkin. Spoon the remaining brownie batter on top, followed by the pumpkin batter and finally the Caramel, if using. Use a knife to gently swirl the mixtures together.

6 Bake for 35–40 minutes until the top is set, the edges are coming away from the tin and a knife inserted should come away moist, but not wet. Remove from the oven, transfer to a wire rack and leave to cool in the tin, before cutting into 15 brownies.

Store for up to 7 days in an airtight container at room temperature or chilled. Suitable for freezing.

FOR THE SALTED CARAMEL SAUCE (OPTIONAL)

150ml (5fl oz) double cream

175g (6oz) golden caster sugar

20g (¾oz) unsalted butter

a pinch of salt

Put the cream in a saucepan and bring to the boil. Remove from the heat and leave to cool slightly. Melt and cook the sugar in a saucepan, with no stirring, until it turns a dark caramel colour. Remove from the heat and add the cream – a little at first as it will bubble up, then pour in the remainder. Add the butter and stir until it has melted. Add salt to taste. Cool and leave to thicken. Store for up to 14 days in a jar in the refrigerator.

5

6

These dairy-free flapjacks can be made with any type of nut butter to add flavour, texture and nutrition without the high fat and refined sugar. Use gluten-free oats and they will be suitable for coeliacs too.

Skinny Peanut Butter Flapjacks

MAKES 16 FLAPJACKS

225g (8oz) Medjool dates, stoned

150ml (5fl oz) water

225g (8oz) crunchy peanut butter
   (or other nut butter, such as
   cashew, hazelnut or almond)

3 large egg whites

175g (6oz) clear honey

600g (1lb 5oz) rolled oats
   (gluten free)

1 Place the dates in a saucepan with the water and simmer until softened and the water has been absorbed. Set aside.

2 Preheat the oven to 160°C/gas 3. Line a 30 x 20cm (12 x 8 inch) tin with non-stick baking parchment.

3 Blend the dates, peanut butter, egg whites and honey together in a food processor or blender until smooth. Stir in the oats until they are well coated.

4 Tip the mixture into the prepared tin and press down firmly. Bake for about 30 minutes until golden. Leave to cool in the tin, then cut into 16 triangles.

Store for up to 5 days in an airtight container at room temperature. Not suitable for freezing.

These blondies have been made with prunes, which are rich in iron and fibre, adding a wonderful natural sweetness. I have added a boost of iron and other vitamins, minerals, flavour and texture with cashew butter and cashews and indulged with the sweetness of white chocolate.

Prune & Cashew Blondies

MAKES 16 BLONDIES

250g (9oz) unsalted butter

250g (9oz) ready-to-eat prunes, stoned and finely chopped

150g (5½oz) golden caster sugar

300g (10½oz) white chocolate, broken into pieces

4 medium eggs, beaten

325g (11¼oz) plain flour

90g (3¼oz) cashew butter

100g (3½oz) chopped cashews

1 Preheat the oven to 180°C/gas 4. Line a 30 x 20cm (12 x 8 inch) tin with non-stick baking parchment.

2 Melt the butter, prunes and sugar in a heavy-based saucepan. Remove from the heat and add the white chocolate whisking well. Leave to cool for 10 minutes. Don't be concerned if the mixture looks split at this stage – once the eggs are added, they will help emulsify the batter.

3 Add the beaten eggs and use a hand balloon whisk to bring everything together to a smooth batter. Add the flour and mix well. Transfer the batter to the prepared tin and level with the back of a spoon.

4 Drop teaspoons of the cashew butter over the blondie base and marble with a knife. Scatter the surface with roughly chopped cashews. Bake for 25–30 minutes until the blondie is baked, golden brown and has a slight wobble.

5 Remove from the oven. Leave to cool on a wire rack. Refrigerate overnight to firm before trimming and cutting into 16 bars.

Store for up to 5 days in an airtight container in the refrigerator. Not suitable for freezing.

VARIATION
Replace the cashew butter and cashews with almond or hazelnut butter and sprinkle with pistachios, pecans or hazelnuts – experiment to find your favourite.

LEFT Banana Granola Flapjacks with apricots and hazelnuts. RIGHT Strawberry and Walnut Flapjacks.

Banana Granola Flapjacks

 F EF

MAKES 24 FLAPJACKS

200g (7oz) unsalted butter

4 tablespoons honey

90g (3¼oz) soft light brown sugar

3 medium ripe bananas

1 large egg

250g (9oz) rolled oats

135g (4¼oz) self-raising flour

75g (2¾oz) chopped dried
   apricots

75g (2¾oz) chopped toasted
   hazelnuts

2 teaspoons ground cinnamon

These flapjack granola bars have been loaded with nutritious goodies including bananas, apricots and hazelnuts. They will provide essential minerals and fibre to the diet and being packed with oats will release energy more slowly, helping to keep you fuller for longer.

1 Preheat the oven to 160°C/gas 3. Line a 30 x 20cm (12 x 8 inch) tin with non-stick baking parchment.

2 Melt the butter, honey and sugar together, then leave to cool. In a separate bowl, mash the bananas with the egg, then stir these into the melted butter and sugar.

3 In a separate bowl, mix the remaining ingredients together.

4 Stir the melted ingredients into the oat mixture and mix until well combined. Tip into the prepared tin and press down firmly.

5 Bake for 30 minutes until golden. Leave to cool in the tin, then cut into 24 squares.

Store for up to 5 days at room temperature in an airtight container. Not suitable for freezing.

Flapjack bars are quick and simple to make. Packed with oats, rich in fibre, vitamins and slow-release carbohydrates, they can be an ideal mid-morning snack cut into small bars. I have included walnuts for extra flavour, texture, protein and essential oils. If you choose gluten-free oats, these will also be perfect for coeliacs.

Strawberry & Walnut Flapjacks

EF GF F

MAKES 24 FLAPJACKS

200g (7oz) unsalted butter

180g (6oz) soft light brown sugar

75g (2¾oz) golden syrup

75g (2¾oz) clear honey

500g (1lb 2oz) rolled oats
(gluten-free oats)

100g (3½oz) chopped walnuts

500g (1lb 2oz) strawberry,
raspberry or mixed berry jam

1 Preheat the oven to 160°C/gas 3. Line a 30 x 20cm (12 x 8 inch) tin with non-stick baking parchment.

2 Melt the butter, sugar, syrup and honey together. Stir in the oats and chopped walnuts.

3 Transfer half the mixture into the prepared tin, press down and spread with the jam. Top with the remaining flapjack mixture and spread with the remaining jam.

4 Bake for 40 minutes until golden. Leave to cool in the tin, then cut into 24 squares.

Store for up to 7 days in an airtight container at room temperature. Not suitable for freezing.

VARIATION
Substitute the walnuts with chopped crystallized ginger, chocolate chips, desiccated coconut or 3 tablespoons peanut, cashew, almond or hazelnut butter.

I have packed these oat bars with dried fruits and nuts and used coconut oil and honey to bind and sweeten. Dairy free, gluten free, no refined sugar – these bars will deliver a satisfying and nutritious hit, and are likely to become a staple in your pantry.

'Who Gives a Fig' Bars

MAKES 16 BARS

200g (7oz) ready-to-eat figs, roughly chopped, with the centre stalks removed

250ml (9fl oz) water

1 tablespoon vanilla bean paste

120g (4½oz) coconut oil

175g (6oz) clear honey

450g (1lb) rolled oats (gluten-free)

75g (2¾oz) sultanas

75g (2¾oz) dried cherries, cranberries or goji berries

115g (4oz) chopped dried apricots

115g (4oz) mixed chopped nuts (hazelnuts, cashews or almonds)

30g (1¼oz) desiccated coconut

1 Preheat the oven to 170°C/gas 3. Line a 30 x 20cm (12 x 8 inch) tin with non-stick baking parchment.

2 Place the figs in a pan with the water and the vanilla bean paste. Gently stew the figs for about 10 minutes until softened. Leave to cool and absorb the liquid, then blitz in a blender to make a paste.

3 In a large saucepan, melt the coconut oil and honey together over a low heat, then stir in the fig paste.

4 Place the remaining ingredients together in a bowl and mix well. Stir the fig batter into the dry ingredients and mix until everything is combined. Tip into the prepared tin and press down firmly.

5 Bake for 30 minutes until golden. Leave to cool in the tin, then chill well before cutting into 16 bars.

Store for up to 5 days in an airtight container at room temperature or chilled. Not suitable for freezing.

How often do you head to the movies and mindlessly munch hand to mouth through a huge bucket of sweet 'n' salty popcorn? Next time, make these ahead of the movies – get the children to join in. They are portion controlled, sweet bars with added crunch and flavour thanks to the coconut, peanuts, raisins and dark chocolate. Better still – they are gluten free and have no added salt.

'Night at The Movies' Popcorn Bar

MAKES 16 BARS

25ml (1fl oz) sunflower oil

80g (2¾oz) popping corn

300g (10½oz) dark chocolate (55–70% cocoa solids), broken into pieces

75g (2¾oz) unsalted butter

125g (4½oz) golden syrup

50g (1¾oz) desiccated coconut

150g (5½oz) roasted peanuts (or sunflower seeds)

150g (5½oz) raisins

1 Line a 30 x 20cm (12 x 8 inch) tin with non-stick baking parchment.

2 Heat the oil in a large saucepan. When the oil is hot, stir in the popping corn. Cover with a tight-fitting lid and cook over a low heat, shaking the pan intermittently until all the kernels have popped.

3 Meanwhile, melt the chocolate, butter and golden syrup together in a microwave or in a heatproof bowl set over a pan of hot water.

4 Toss the popcorn, coconut, nuts and raisins with the chocolate and pour into the prepared tin. Press down firmly and chill for about 4–6 hours until set. Turn out of the tin and use a sharp knife to chop into 16 bars.

Store for up to 3 days in an airtight container at room temperature or chilled. Not suitable for freezing.

These oat slices have been a stalwart throughout the years – we always have a batch available – for just when you are looking for a little something. Enormously satisfying for breakfast, morning coffee or with an afternoon cup of tea – even a glass of milk before bed! Try adding sunflower seeds, flaxseeds, cinnamon, chopped cashews or almonds to the oat base to find your personal favourite. High in fibre, with oats and iron-rich fruits, nuts and seeds.

Oaty Date Slice

MAKES 16 SLICES

250g (9oz) plain flour

115g (4oz) wholemeal flour

115g (4oz) soft light brown sugar

165g (5¾oz) rolled porridge oats

250g (9oz) unsalted butter, melted

500g (1lb 2oz) Medjool dates, stoned and roughly chopped

grated zest of 2 lemons

150ml (5fl oz) water

1 Preheat the oven to 180°C/gas 4. Line the base and sides 30 x 20cm (12 x 8 inch) tin with non-stick baking parchment.

2 Measure the flours, sugar and oats into a bowl and mix. Make a well in the centre and pour in the melted butter. Mix together to form an oaty, crumbly mixture.

3 Put the dates in a saucepan with the lemon zest and water. Heat over a medium-high heat until the dates have softened and the water has been absorbed. Press half the oat mixture into the base of the tin and press down firmly. Spread the date mixture over the base, then top with the remaining oat mixture. Press down firmly.

4 Bake for 35–40 minutes until golden. Remove from the oven. Leave to cool in the tin, then cut into 16 slices.

Store for up to 5 days in an airtight container at room temperature or chilled. Not suitable for freezing.

VARIATION

Substitute the dates for unsulphured apricots – these have a wonderful caramelized flavour – and add 50g (1¾oz) sunflower seeds and 50g (1¾oz) chopped cashews to the oat base, for a boost of fibre and iron.

TOP TIP

Dried apricots are treated with sulphur dioxide to retain their orange colouring, which destroys the vitamin B1 content. Look instead for unsulphured or organic apricots – these will be darker brown in colour as they have been naturally dried. They will be more caramelized and sweeter in flavour, with a less pronounced sharp tangy flavour and will retain their vitamin B1 content (the packets are usually sealed so as not to show their supposedly less desirable darker brown colour).

'The Power of Three'

Is it a cookie? Is it a brownie? Is it a coconut
macaroon? It's all three! The perfect choice when
your willpower needs a helping hand – rather
than three separate bakes – you get to have all
three in one! These bite-sized squares are a
huge hit with our clientele in The Middle East.
Wonderfully sweet and decadent with layers
of peanut butter cookie, chocolate brownie and
coconut macaroon, I have used unrefined sugar
throughout and no added salt. These squares are
the real deal – save for super special occasions as
they are uber addictive.

MAKES 40 BITE-SIZED SQUARES

FOR THE COOKIE LAYER

450ml (16fl oz) smooth peanut
butter

300g (10½oz) golden caster sugar

2 medium eggs

1 teaspoon pure vanilla extract

110g (3¾oz) plain flour

FOR THE BROWNIE LAYER

250g (9oz) plain flour

65g (2¼oz) cocoa powder

150g (5½oz) unsalted butter

115g (4oz) dark chocolate (70%
cocoa solids), chopped

225g (8oz) soft light brown sugar

3 large eggs, lightly beaten

125g (4½oz) milk chocolate chips

FOR THE MACAROON LAYER

3 large egg whites

300g (10½oz) desiccated coconut

55g (2oz) golden caster sugar

1 teaspoon pure vanilla extract

1 Preheat the oven to 160°C/gas 3. Line the base and sides of a 30 x 20cm (12 x 8 inch) tin with non-stick baking parchment.

2 For the cookie layer, beat the peanut butter and sugar together until smooth. Beat the eggs in one at a time, then the vanilla. Add the flour and beat until just incorporated. Press the dough into an even layer in the bottom of the prepared tin. Set aside.

3 For the brownie layer, combine the flour and cocoa powder in a medium bowl, then set aside. Melt the butter and chopped chocolate in a saucepan over a medium heat, stirring, until smooth. Remove from the heat, leave to cool slightly, then stir in the sugar. Mix in the eggs until combined. Stir in the flour mixture, then the chocolate chips until just combined. Pour the brownie mix over the cookie layer and spread to the edges.

4 For the macaroon layer, whisk the egg whites in a large bowl until frothy. Toss the coconut, sugar and vanilla together with your hands in a separate bowl. Add the egg whites and stir until the coconut mixture is coated. Scatter the coconut mixture in an even layer to completely cover the brownie layer.

5 Bake for 1 hour until the top layer is golden and the tin has a gentle wobble when shaken. (You can't use the knife insertion test here – if a knife came out clean the bars would be overbaked.) If the coconut is darkening too much, cover lightly with foil.

6 Transfer the tin to a wire rack and leave to cool completely, preferably overnight. Lift it out of the tin and peel away the paper. Trim the bar with a sharp knife to make neat edges and cut into 40 very small squares, about 3.5cm (1½ inch) square.

Store for 7 days in an airtight container at room temperature. Not suitable for freezing.

2

3

Carrots and pumpkin are both rich sources of beta-carotene – a protective antioxidant and contain 0% fat. These bars will provide added vitamins, minerals and fibre. Quick and easy to make, these bars are great for packed lunches and picnics or to have on the go. I have swirled an optional cream cheese frosting into the bar before baking for added flavour, which means they can be stored in the refrigerator and transported at room temperature.

Pumpkin & Carrot Bars

MAKES 16 BARS

300g (10½oz) plain flour

2 teaspoons bicarbonate of soda

2 teaspoons ground cinnamon

1 teaspoon ground ginger

1 teaspoon ground nutmeg

150ml (5fl oz) sunflower oil

3 large eggs

275g (9¾oz) soft light brown sugar

1 x tin (400g/14oz) pumpkin purée

100g (3½oz) grated carrot

FOR THE TOPPING

115g (4oz) cream cheese, room temperature

60g (2¼oz) golden caster sugar

2 teaspoons vanilla extract

1 Preheat the oven to 180°C/gas 4. Line the base and sides of a 30 x 20cm (12 x 8 inch) tin with non-stick baking parchment.

2 Combine the flour, raising agent and spices together in a bowl and set aside. Combine the oil, eggs and sugar until smooth. Stir in the flour mixture followed by the pumpkin purée and grated carrot. Pour into the prepared tin.

3 For the cream cheese frosting, beat the ingredients together until smooth. Drop spoonfuls over the carrot and pumpkin batter and use a knife to swirl.

4 Bake for 25–30 minutes until a knife inserted comes out clean. Remove from the oven. Leave to cool, then cut into 16 bars.

Store for 3–5 days in an airtight container in the refrigerator. Suitable for freezing.

Moist and delicious Pumpkin and Carrot Bars.

Ginger is a flowering plant with a distinctive rhizome – and the root part has been used for culinary and ayurvedic purposes for centuries. It has a distinctive flavour, rich in B vitamins, iron and manganese, which is essential for development, metabolism and as part of the body's antioxidant process. Ginger is well known to combat nausea – especially morning sickness and sea sickness. It can be productive in stimulating digestion, absorption and elimination, adding a boost to the body's natural metabolism. This shortbread includes fresh and crystallized ginger for a double hit and is made with wholemeal flour for increased fibre. This shortbread improves with keeping, but it is essential not to overmix it – this is one where the magic really does happen in the oven. If it is overmixed, it is like a brick and you could build houses with it!

ginger shortbread

MAKES 16 SQUARES

350g (12oz) soft dark brown sugar

350g (12oz) unsalted butter, softened

1 level teaspoon bicarbonate of soda

4cm (1½ inch) piece of ginger, peeled and grated

40g (1½oz) chopped crystallized ginger

500g (1lb 2oz) plain wholemeal flour

demerara sugar, for sprinkling

1 Preheat the oven to 160°C/gas 3. Line the base and sides of a 30 x 20cm (12 x 8 inch) tin with non-stick baking parchment.

2 Put the sugar, butter, bicarbonate of soda and both gingers in a bowl and stir with a wooden spoon until just mixed (do not beat). Add the flour and mix until it just starts to cling together.

3 Place the mixture in the prepared tin, press down firmly and level the surface with the back of a metal spoon. Sprinkle liberally with demerara sugar and press lightly with the back of the spoon again.

4 Bake in the centre of the oven for about 1 hour until the shortbread is dark brown in colour, firm in the centre and beginning to shrink away from the side of the tin.

5 Leave to cool in the tin for 10 minutes, then cut into 16 squares with a sharp knife. Leave for a further 15 minutes, then turn out onto a wire rack to cool completely.

Store for up to 7 days in an airtight container at room temperature. Not suitable for freezing.

2

3

Enjoy a double hit of
ginger with these Ginger
Shortbread Squares.

Cakes

'If I knew you were coming I'd have baked a cake!' and more often than not – I would! Baking a cake for someone – friends or family, work colleagues or charity event – is a wonderful, pleasurable thing to do. It fills you with self-pride, a sense of achievement and builds confidence. In this chapter I have included a selection of wonderful delicious, nutritious cakes to bake for every occasion, to have on the go and enjoy at any time of the day. Packed full of additional nutritional ingredients to offer variety, flavour, texture and choice, these cakes range from the very simple batter or loaf cakes for the beginner to the more technically challenging, roulades and layered cakes with fillings and frostings for the more adventurous baker.

Carrot Cake with Orange Cream Cheese Frosting & Walnut Praline

This is the recipe I created for the wedding of Pierce Brosnan and Keely Shaye Smith. It is wonderfully moist, with a delicious blend of carrots, fruit and spices. Because the cake is made with sunflower oil it is naturally dairy free and can be served chilled. I have decorated it here with a velvet soft cream cheese frosting and caramelized walnut praline for added flavour, texture, sweetness and crunch.

MAKES A 20CM (8 INCH) ROUND CAKE

4 large eggs

300ml (10fl oz) sunflower oil

150g (5½oz) golden caster sugar

150g (5½oz) soft light brown sugar

350g (12oz) plain flour

1 tablespoon ground cinnamon

2 teaspoons ground nutmeg

2 teaspoons bicarbonate of soda

40g (1½oz) stem ginger

grated zest of 2 oranges

grated zest of 2 lemons

100g (3½oz) walnuts, chopped

100g (3½oz) desiccated coconut

200g (7oz) sultanas soaked in 50ml (2fl oz) rum for 1 hour

350g (12oz) carrots, peeled and grated

FOR THE SYRUP

150g (5½oz) soft light brown sugar

juice of 2 lemons

juice of 2 oranges

FOR THE CREAM CHEESE FROSTING

75g (2¾oz) unsalted butter, slightly softened

450g (1lb) icing sugar

190g (6¾oz) full fat cream cheese, chilled

grated zest of 1 orange

FOR THE WALNUT PRALINE

150g (5½oz) golden caster sugar

100g (3½oz) walnuts, roughly chopped and roasted (see page 94 for how to roast nuts)

VARIATION

Replace the orange zest with 1 tablespoon vanilla bean paste for a vanilla cream cheese frosting. Or use a dairy-free buttercream made from soya spread and icing sugar flavoured with fresh orange zest for a totally dairy-free cake.

1 Preheat the oven to 150°C/gas 2. Line the base and sides of a deep sided 20cm (8 inch) cake tin with non-stick baking parchment.

2 Blend together the eggs, oil and sugars until well mixed. In a separate bowl, sift the flour, spices and bicarbonate of soda together and stir into the oil mixture to create a smooth batter.

3 Add the remaining ingredients until well mixed and spoon into the prepared cake tin. Bake for 2 hours until well risen, golden brown and a knife inserted in the centre comes out clean.

4 As soon as the cake is in the oven, prepare the syrup. Measure the ingredients into a jug and stir until dissolved.

5 As soon as the cake is baked, place it on a wire rack, spike over the entire cake with a skewer and pour over all the syrup. Leave the cake to completely cool in the tin.

6 To make the cream cheese frosting, rub the butter into the icing sugar to resemble fine breadcrumbs. Add the chilled cream cheese and beat until smooth. Stir in the orange zest.

CREAM CHEESE FROSTING

6

7 To make the praline, line a baking sheet with non-stick baking parchment. Put the sugar in a heavy-based pan over a medium heat until the sugar melts and turns a warm caramel colour. Add the roasted walnuts, stir until well coated, then transfer to the prepared baking sheet. Leave to cool, then blitz in a food processor or blender, or chop with a knife, into small bite-sized pieces.

8 Turn the cooled cake out of the tin and use a palette knife to surround the top and sides of the cake with the cream cheese frosting. Use a side scraper to professionally smooth the sides of the cake. Sprinkle the top with the walnut praline and refrigerate to set.

Store for up to 7 days in an airtight container in the refrigerator. Serve at room temperature. Suitable for freezing.

WALNUT PRALINE

7

ASSEMBLING THE CAKE

8

Dried fruits have a higher concentration of natural fruit sugar and offer additional nutrients such as minerals and fibre to cakes and bakes. In this chocolate cake, the prunes add texture, help keep the cake moist and add natural sweetness so I have reduced the overall sugar and have used ground almonds so this cake is also gluten free.

Chocolate Cake with Prunes

MAKES A 20CM (8 INCH) ROUND CAKE

140g (5oz) prunes, softened, ready-to-eat variety, stoned

4 tablespoons water (80ml/3fl oz)

2 teaspoons vanilla extract

100g (3½oz) unsalted butter, plus extra for greasing

150g (5½oz) dark chocolate (70% cocoa solids), broken into pieces

150g (5½oz) golden caster sugar

4 large eggs – 2 whole and 2 separated

125g (4½oz) ground almonds

cocoa powder, for dusting

1 Preheat the oven to 170°C/gas 3. Gently stew the prunes with the water and vanilla extract over a low heat until hot. Remove from the heat, cover and allow to absorb the liquid. Blitz the entire contents in a food processor or blender to make a smooth paste.

2 Grease the base and sides of a 20cm (8 inch) springform cake tin. Line the base with non-stick baking parchment and dust the sides with cocoa powder.

3 Melt the butter and chocolate together in a heatproof bowl over a pan of simmering water. Stir in the prune paste.

4 Whisk the sugar, eggs and egg yolks together until thick, pale and doubled in volume. Fold the chocolate mixture into the egg mixture, then sift in the ground almonds. Fold until well combined. Whisk the remaining 2 egg whites until stiff but not dry. Gently fold into the cake batter in 3 additions.

5 Spoon into the prepared tin and bake for 20–25 minutes until the cake has crusted over. Remove from the oven and transfer to a wire rack. Leave the cake to completely cool in the tin – it will sink back and likely crack as it does so. Chill the cake until firm for easier handling.

6 Remove the cake from the tin, dust with additional cocoa powder and leave to come up to room temperature before serving.

Best eaten on the day it is made, although will keep for 2–3 days at room temperature, loosely covered. Not suitable for freezing.

This is the go-to favourite cake in our house. I developed this recipe with Her Majesty the Queen in mind. It combines dates with apples, fresh lemon and ginger. The combination of brown sugars results in a rich, caramelized flavour, which balances well with the acidity of the apples and lemon. The apples provide natural sweetness and a great source of fibre.

Queen Elizabeth Date Cake

MAKES A 20CM (8 INCH) ROUND CAKE

200g (7oz) unsalted butter

135g (4¼oz) light muscovado brown sugar

135g (4¼oz) dark muscovado sugar

250g (9oz) Medjool dates (I use 12), each one stoned and roughly chopped into 4 pieces

100g (3½oz) sultanas

2 large eggs

250g (9oz) self-raising flour

250g (9oz) Bramley apples, peeled, cored and grated (I tend to use 2 medium-large size apples. It is OK if it is just over 250g/9oz, this will just make the cake more moist, with more of a pudding texture)

grated zest of 2 lemons

2.5cm (1 inch) piece of ginger, peeled and grated

1 Preheat the oven to 160°C/gas 3. Line the base and sides of a 20cm (8 inch) round tin with non-stick baking parchment.

2 Put the butter and sugars in a large saucepan and heat over a medium heat until melted. Stir in the chopped dates and sultanas and continue to heat over a low heat for about 10 minutes until the dates and sultanas soften. Remove the pan from the heat and leave to cool.

3 Stir the eggs into the cooled mixture and mix with a wooden spoon. Stir in the flour until well mixed. Stir in the grated apple, lemon zest and ginger until well mixed, then tip into the prepared tin. Bake for 1 hour 15 minutes until risen and golden brown.

4 Leave to cool in the tin for 5 minutes, then turn out onto a wire rack to cool. This cake can be served warm with vanilla ice cream, crème fraîche or Greek-style yogurt or cooled with a cup of coffee.

Store for up to 7 days in an airtight container at room temperature. Suitable for freezing.

VARIATION

If you are wanting to reduce the wheat flour content, substitute 50g (1¾oz) of the flour with coconut flour and add 1 teaspoon baking powder.

Nutritious, delicious with no refined sugar and no added salt. This cake is deliciously moist, full of flavour and texture with fibre from the courgettes and pecans. It has an earthy, buttery flavour, which balances beautifully with the zesty sweetness of the optional lemon drizzle icing.

'Zucchini Pikini, into your Bikini' Cake

MAKES A 23CM (9 INCH) ROUND CAKE

300g (10½oz) unsalted butter, plus extra for greasing

300g (10½oz) plain flour, plus extra for dusting

300g (10½oz) golden caster sugar

3 medium eggs

340g (11½oz) grated courgettes

1 teaspoon baking powder

3 teaspoons ground cinnamon

100g (3½oz) chopped pecans

120g (4¼oz) sultanas

grated zest of 2 lemons

60g (2¼oz) chopped roasted pecans (see page 94 for how to roast nuts)

FOR THE LEMON DRIZZLE

100g (3½oz) golden icing sugar

juice of 1 lemon

1 Preheat the oven to 180°C/gas 4. Butter and flour a 23cm (9 inch) ring mould.

2 Cream the butter and sugar until pale and light. Add the eggs slowly until fully mixed

3 Grate the courgettes, squeeze them gently with your hands to remove some of the moisture, then add to the creamed mixture.

4 In a separate bowl, measure and mix the flour, baking powder and cinnamon and gently fold into the creamed batter. Stir in the pecans, sultanas and lemon zest.

5 Spoon the batter into the prepared tin and bake in the oven for 50–60 minutes until golden, firm to the touch and a knife inserted in the centre comes out clean. Transfer to a wire rack and leave to cool for 10 minutes in the tin before turning out to cool completely.

6 To make the drizzle, sift the icing sugar into a bowl and add the lemon juice through a tea strainer or sieve. Mix and adjust to the right consistency. Spoon into a piping bag and snip the end. Drizzle the icing over the cake and decorate with roasted, chopped pecans.

Store for 3–5 days, covered, at room temperature or chilled. Suitable for freezing.

6

This cake is made with double cream rather than butter. At 46 percent fat, rather than 80 percent, the cake will be lower in overall fat. It is delicately flavoured with vanilla and a hint of lemon. With lower fat, it is best eaten on the day it is baked, served with fresh fruit compote (see page 19).

Lemon Cream Cake

MAKES A 20CM (8 INCH) ROUND CAKE

groundnut oil or butter, for greasing

230g (8¼oz) plain flour

1 lightly heaped teaspoon baking powder

3 large eggs, separated

200g (7oz) icing sugar

230ml (8fl oz) double cream

grated zest of 1 lemon

1 teaspoon vanilla powder (or 2 teaspoons vanilla bean paste)

vanilla sugar, for dusting

1 Preheat the oven to 180°C/gas 4. Grease and line the base and sides of a 20cm (8 inch) round springform cake tin.

2 Sift together the flour and baking powder. Place the egg yolks and sugar together in a bowl and whisk until thick and aerated. Beat in the cream slowly until just mixed, but do not overbeat. Fold in the flour, lemon zest and vanilla powder.

3 Whisk the egg whites until they reach the soft peak stage and fold into the cake batter with a metal spoon. Pour the batter into the prepared tin and place in the oven. Immediately reduce the temperature to 170°C/gas 3 and bake for 50–60 minutes until risen, golden brown and a skewer inserted comes out clean.

4 Remove from the oven and transfer to a wire rack. Leave to cool for 10 minutes in the tin, then turn out and leave to cool completely. Dust with vanilla sugar.

Best eaten on the day it is made. Not suitable for freezing.

For those on a gluten-free diet, polenta is the winner, as it's made from ground cornmeal. It is low in fat, less than 1g per 100g (3½oz) with 0% cholesterol. It is a rich source of iron (for energy and healthy blood, hair, skin and nails) and beta-carotene (a powerful antioxidant). This citrus and elderflower cake is served with a combination of fresh fruit and jam, for a 'best of both worlds' sweetness combined with acidity.

Lemon Polenta Cake with Strawberry Compote

 GF

MAKES A 20CM (8 INCH) ROUND CAKE

250g (9oz) unsalted butter, plus extra for greasing

250g (9oz) golden caster sugar

3 large eggs

100g (3½oz) polenta

250g (9oz) ground almonds

1 teaspoon baking powder (gluten-free)

grated zest of 3 lemons

45ml (1½fl oz) citrus juice (squeezed from the zested lemons)

40ml (1½fl oz) elderflower cordial

FOR THE TOPPING

170g (6oz) strawberry jam

350g (12oz) strawberries, hulled and quartered

grated zest and juice of 1 lime

1 Preheat the oven to 160°C/gas 3. Grease and line the base of a non-stick 20cm (8 inch) springform cake tin.

2 Cream the butter and sugar together until light and fluffy. Add the eggs slowly until fully combined.

3 In a separate bowl, combine the polenta, ground almonds and baking powder. Carefully fold the dry ingredients into the cake batter until mixed. Add the zest and juice and elderflower cordial and stir until well mixed.

4 Pour the batter into the prepared tin and bake for 50 minutes or until the cake has risen and is golden on top. Remove from the oven, transfer to a wire rack and leave to cool in the tin.

5 To prepare the topping, place the strawberry jam in a heavy-based saucepan and bring to the boil. Simmer the jam for 3 minutes, then add the quartered strawberries and lime zest and juice. Simmer for a further 2 minutes. Remove the strawberry compote from the heat, transfer to a clean jug and set aside to cool.

6 To serve, place the cake on a plate and spread the compote over the whole cake before serving.

Store for up to 3 days loosely covered with cling film in the refrigerator. Not suitable for freezing.

Plum & Nectarine Upside-down Cake

Adding fresh fruit to cakes will naturally sweeten the cake, help to keep it moist and add nutritional value. This cake is wonderful for using fruits as they come in to season. Fresh pineapple, apricots, plums, nectarines, peaches and pears can all be used. Natural sources of fibre, vitamins, minerals and low in fat – and with more fruit and less cake, you can certainly have your cake and eat it!

MAKES A 25CM (10 INCH) CAKE

190g (6¾oz) softened unsalted
   butter

190g (6¾oz) golden caster sugar

190g (6¾oz) self-raising flour

1½ teaspoons baking powder

3 teaspoons vanilla bean paste

3 large eggs (weighing about
   125g/4½oz)

60ml (3fl oz) whole milk

FOR THE TOPPING

75g (2¾oz) softened unsalted
   butter

75g (2¾oz) soft light brown sugar

3 ripe nectarines, stoned –
   2 quartered and 1 halved

4–6 ripe plums, stoned and
   quartered

1 Preheat the oven to 180°C/gas 4. Line the base and sides of a 25cm (10 inch) deep sandwich tin with non-stick baking parchment.

2 For the topping, beat the butter and sugar together until creamy and spread over the base and a quarter of the way up the sides of the cake tin.

3 Spread the nectarines and plums over the base.

4 For the cake, place all the ingredients in a bowl and beat for about 5 minutes until light and fluffy. Spoon the batter over the fruit and level the surface with the back of a spoon.

5 Bake for 35 minutes until golden and risen. Remove from the oven and transfer to a wire rack. Leave to cool in the tin for 10 minutes, then turn out onto a cake plate. Serve warm with unsweetened Greek-style yogurt, if liked.

Best eaten fresh on the day it is made. Not suitable for freezing.

VARIATION
Add chopped stem ginger or freshly grated ginger to the cake batter for added flavour.

2

3

4

This cake is perfect when you are looking for a showstopper 'naked' gateau to please all palates with additional ingredients to ensure the cake is nutritious and delicious. I have added ground almonds to boost the nutritional content and fresh citrus zests and coconut to add flavour.

Citrus Coconut Layered Cake

MAKES A LAYERED 20CM (8 INCH) CAKE

550g (1lb 4oz) unsalted butter, at room temperature, plus extra for greasing

550g (1lb 4oz) golden caster sugar

9 medium eggs (total weight about 500g/1lb 2oz), beaten

400g (14oz) ground almonds

150g (5½oz) plain flour

100g (3½oz) desiccated coconut

2 teaspoons baking powder

grated zest of 2 lemons, 2 limes and 2 oranges

150g (5½oz) Lime Curd (see page 18), for filling

frosted rosemary sprigs and redcurrants (see page 184), to decorate

FOR THE SYRUP

75ml (2½fl oz) mixed lemon, lime and orange juice

75g (2¾oz) golden caster sugar

FOR THE COCONUT BUTTERCREAM FROSTING

125g (4½oz) unsalted butter, softened

265g (9¼oz) icing sugar

2 tablespoons coconut cream

1 Preheat the oven to 170°C/gas 3. Grease and line 2 x 20cm (8 inch) deep cake tins with non-stick baking parchment. Cream together the butter and sugar until light and fluffy. Add the beaten eggs slowly, beating well after each addition.

2 In a separate bowl, mix together the almonds, flour, coconut and baking powder. Fold into the creamed mixture until even and smooth and stir in the citrus zests. Spoon into the prepared tins, level the surface and bake for 50 minutes until lightly golden and when pressed, spring back. Remove from the oven and transfer to a wire rack. Leave in the tin for 10 minutes, then turn the cakes out to cool completely. Chill for at least 4 hours until firm.

3 To make the syrup, blend the mixed juice with the sugar in a saucepan. Warm gently until the sugar dissolves. To make the buttercream, beat the butter and sugar together, then stir in the coconut cream.

4 To decorate, slice the 2 cakes in half horizontally, then brush each half with the syrup on the cut side. Place the first sponge on a serving plate and spread with half the Lime Curd. Place a second sponge on top and spread with a thin layer of coconut buttercream using a palette knife. Layer the third cake and spread with the remaining curd.

5 Place the final sponge in position and spread the remaining frosting around the sides and top of the cake and use a palette knife or cake scraper to scrape off the excess to leave a naked and rustic finish. Dress the cake with sprigs of rosemary and frosted redcurrants.

Store for up to 5 days loosely covered with cling film at room temperature or chilled. Not suitable for freezing.

Roulades always look impressive and are deceptively easy to make – once you know how! They are made by the whisking method and contain little if any fat, making them a good choice for those looking to reduce their fat, cholesterol and calorie intake. I have chosen to fill this gluten-free roulade with a coffee cream, made with double or whipping cream, both of which are lower in fat than butter.

Chocolate & Coffee Roulade

 GF LF

SERVES 8

6 large eggs, separated

150g (5½oz) golden caster sugar, plus extra for dusting

50g (1¾oz) cocoa powder, plus extra for dusting

FOR THE FILLING

300ml (10fl oz) double or whipping cream

75g (2¾oz) golden icing sugar

3 tablespoons espresso coffee, cooled

30g (1¼oz) chocolate-covered coffee beans, finely chopped

TO DECORATE

10g (¼oz) roughly chopped, chocolate-covered coffee beans

1 Preheat the oven to 180°C/gas 4. Line the base and sides of a 30 x 20cm (12 x 8 inch) Swiss roll tin with non-stick baking parchment.

2 Place the egg yolks and sugar in a large heatproof bowl set over a saucepan of barely simmering water and whisk with an electric hand whisk until the mixture has tripled in size, is light and voluminous and leaves a ribbon trail across the surface when lifted.

3 Sift in the cocoa and fold it through carefully with a metal spoon or balloon whisk.

4 In a separate bowl, whisk the egg whites to a soft peak. Fold the egg whites into the batter in 3 stages. It is important to fold the egg whites in gently to ensure they are evenly incorporated, but not to knock out the air, so take your time.

5 Pour the batter into the prepared tin and spread out to the corners. Bake for 15–20 minutes until risen and the surface springs back when gently pressed.

Continued overleaf...

VARIATION
To make this completely dairy free, fill the roulade with a non-dairy cream, such as soya cream.

6 Meanwhile, soak a clean tea towel in cold water, wring out well and lay on a clean work surface. Cover with a sheet of non-stick baking parchment dusted with cocoa powder and sugar.

7 As soon as the roulade is baked, remove from the oven, invert onto the cocoa sugar dusted paper and carefully remove the parchment by tearing in strips. Roll the roulade up from the short end, keeping the non-stick baking parchment inside, then wrapping inside the tea towel. The chilled, damp tea towel will help set the roulade in its curled position, helping to prevent cracks when it is unrolled. Set aside to cool for 1 hour.

8 To make the filling, combine the cream, icing sugar and espresso in a bowl. Taste and adjust the coffee or sugar to taste. Whip the cream to soft peaks. Fill a large piping bag with an open star nozzle and 3 large tablespoons of the coffee cream and set aside.

9 Unroll the roulade, spread the remaining coffee cream over the surface of the roulade using a palette knife. Sprinkle with the chocolate coffee beans. Roll up tightly using the parchment to assist. Dust with more cocoa powder if desired. Lift onto a serving plate with the seam underneath, then remove the parchment. To decorate, hand pipe the coffee cream on top and scatter with chopped chocolate coffee beans.

Store for 2 days in the refrigerator, but it is best eaten the day it is made.

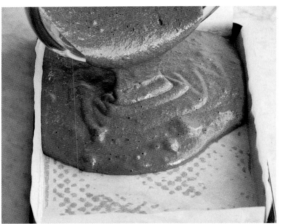

5

7

8

Pine nuts are rich in essential fatty acids, which are good for boosting heart health. They satisfy the appetite as well as offering texture, flavour and taste. Combined with a lower-fat sponge, this is delicious and impressive. Enjoy!

Pine Nut & Passion Fruit Roulade

SERVES 8

30g (1¼oz) unsalted butter

4 medium eggs

115g (4oz) golden caster sugar, plus extra for dusting

2 tablespoons vanilla bean paste

grated zest of 1 lemon

115g (4oz) plain flour

100g (3½oz) pine nuts

25g (1oz) toasted pine nuts, to decorate

FOR THE FILLING

½ quantity of Crème Chantilly (see page 180)

½ quantity of Passion Fruit Curd (see page 18)

1 Preheat the oven to 180°C/gas 4. Line a 30 x 20cm (12 x 8 inch) Swiss roll tin with non-stick baking parchment.

2 Melt the butter and set aside to cool. Place the eggs and sugar in a large bowl and whisk for about 5 minutes until the mixture forms a thick trail, then briefly whisk in the vanilla bean paste and lemon zest. Sift the flour into the mixture and gently fold in with a metal spoon. Drizzle in the cooled, melted butter around the edge of the bowl and gently fold in until well mixed.

3 Transfer the batter to the prepared tin, level with the back of a metal spoon and scatter the surface with pine nuts. Bake for 10–12 minutes until risen, golden brown and springy to the touch.

4 Soak a tea towel with cold water and place on a clean work surface. Place a sheet of non-stick baking parchment on top, dusted lightly with golden caster sugar. Invert the roulade onto the baking parchment and remove the baking parchment in strips as shown on page 156. Roll the roulade up tightly, keeping the fresh baking parchment inside and wrapped in the tea towel. Set aside to cool.

5 Once cooled, unravel the roulade. Use a palette knife to spread the roulade evenly with Crème Chantilly. Drizzle the Passion Fruit Curd over the surface. Carefully roll the roulade up and transfer to a serving plate. Decorate with the toasted pine nuts to serve.

Best eaten fresh on the day it is made. Not suitable for freezing.

VARIATION
Substitute the pine nuts for other nuts, such as pistachios, almonds or chopped hazelnuts. Try other citrus curds to find your favourites.

Heavenly Vanilla Cake

This has to be the ultimate vanilla cake to include in your repertoire. It is a to-die-for-cake that never fails to impress. It is important not to rush any of the stages. This cake is made with butter and spiked with a vanilla syrup as soon as it is baked. The Swiss meringue buttercream is lower in sugar than regular buttercream. I have chosen to flavour it with freeze-dried blackcurrant powder, which adds an intensity of flavour without adding any additional sugar or artificial colour. One of the secrets is the quality of the ingredients, which showcase the flavour of vanilla bean paste. The result is a nostalgic vanilla cake that quite literally nurtures the soul. Food for the Gods!

MAKES A 20CM (8 INCH) ROUND CAKE OR 2 X 15CM (6 INCH) CAKES

420g (14¾oz) self-raising flour

300g (10½oz) golden caster sugar

300g (10½oz) unsalted butter, softened

6 large eggs, beaten

120ml (4fl oz) semi-skimmed milk

3 tablespoons vanilla bean paste

FOR THE SYRUP

150ml (5fl oz) water

150g (5½oz) golden caster sugar

1 tablespoon vanilla extract

FOR THE SWISS MERINGUE BUTTERCREAM

225ml (8fl oz) egg whites, at room temperature (about 6 eggs)

400g (14oz) caster sugar

565g (1lb 4oz) unsalted butter

3 teaspoons vanilla bean paste

4–6 tablespoons freeze-dried blackcurrant powder

1 Preheat the oven to 160°C/gas 3. Line a deep 20cm (8 inch) round cake tin or 2 x 15cm (6 inch) cake tins with non-stick baking parchment.

2 To make the syrup, put the water, sugar and vanilla in a pan, heat gently until the sugar dissolves, stirring all the time, then remove from the heat.

3 Cream together the butter and sugar until light and fluffy. Add the eggs a little at a time, beating well between each addition. Fold the flour into the creamed mixture. Stir in the milk and the vanilla bean paste.

4 Spoon the batter into the prepared tin and bake for 1½ hours (or 1 hour for the smaller cakes) or until golden colour and a skewer inserted in the centre comes out clean.

5 Remove from the oven and pierce the cake with a skewer several times. Pour the syrup over the cake. Cool, then chill in the tin before removing.

6 To make the buttercream, place the egg whites and the sugar in a large clean heatproof bowl over a pan of gently simmering water. Whisk with a hand balloon whisk and monitor the temperature until your reach 61–70°C (142–158°F). This will take about 10 minutes.

7 Remove the meringue from the heat, attach the bowl to an electric whisk and continue to whisk until the meringue cools to room temperature and has thickened. Add the butter in batches and beat well between each addition. Add the vanilla and whisk until combined.

8 Blend half the buttercream with the blackcurrant powder. Stir well, leave to stand for 1 hour, then stir again.

9 Cut each of the cakes in half and sandwich together with the buttercream. Place on a round cake board, skim coat the cakes with blackcurrant buttercream and place on a pretty cake stand.

10 Fill a large piping bag with a 2D nozzle and pipe a row of buttercream roses around the base of the cake making sure to cover the base board and keeping the roses even.

11 Empty the piping bag back into the bowl along with any remaining blackcurrant buttercream and add one-third of the remaining plain buttercream to this. Stir to create a paler blackcurrant buttercream. Fill the bag with this and pipe a second row of roses around the middle of the cake. Repeat this process and pipe the top ring of roses with a paler shade again. Combine all the remaining buttercream to achieve the palest colour of all and pipe roses on the top of the cake, starting from the outside and working your way in.

Store for up to 5 days in the refrigerator. Serve at room temperature. Not suitable for freezing.

LEFT Fresh blueberries are the star of this Soured Cream Vanilla and Blueberry Cake.
RIGHT Skinnylicious Vanilla Cake – FAT FREE – this vanilla sponge is layered with Italian meringue and berry compote.

Soured Cream Vanilla & Blueberry Cake

With cream being about half the fat of butter, a vanilla cake made with soured cream can be a lovely recipe to consider as a healthier option, especially if the cake is baked with fruit inside for added flavour and moistness. Here I have included a cake baked with soured cream, blueberries, then topped with a cream-based frosting and seasonal berries.

MAKES A 23CM (9 INCH) ROUND CAKE

225g (8oz) unsalted butter, softened, plus extra for greasing

225g (8oz) golden caster sugar

4 medium eggs

1 tablespoon vanilla bean paste

285g (10oz) self-raising flour

1½ teaspoons baking powder

100ml (3½fl oz) soured cream

250g (9oz) blueberries

FOR THE FROSTING

150g (5½oz) cream cheese

75g (2¾oz) icing sugar

1 teaspoon vanilla bean paste

60ml (2½fl oz) soured cream

1 Preheat the oven to 160°C/gas 3. Grease and line the base and sides of a 23cm (9 inch) round springform tin.

2 Cream the butter and sugar until light and fluffy, then add the beaten eggs a little at a time, beating well between each addition. Stir in the vanilla bean paste.

3 Sift the flour and baking powder together, then fold into the creamed mixture. Stir in the soured cream, then finally fold in 150g (5½oz) of the blueberries.

4 Spoon the batter into the prepared tin and level with the back of a spoon. Bake for 1 hour until risen, golden and a skewer inserted comes out clean.

5 Remove the cake from the oven and transfer to a wire rack. Leave the cake to cool in the tin for 5–10 minutes, then turn out and leave to cool. Chill for 2 hours, then place the cake on a cake plate.

6 To make the frosting, beat the cream cheese, icing sugar, vanilla and soured cream together until smooth and spread over the surface of the chilled cake. Decorate with the remaining blueberries and chill for 2 hours to set. Leave the cake to come up to room temperature for 1 hour prior to serving.

Store for 2–3 days, covered, in the refrigerator. Serve at room temperature. Not suitable for freezing.

From one extreme to the other – this vanilla cake is made by the whisking method, using eggs, sugar and flour with NO FAT AT ALL. It will be wonderfully light and aerated and is best enjoyed on the day it is made. I have layered this cake with a smooth Italian meringue and fresh berry compote. Surprisingly light you can almost feel the halo as you eat it!

Skinnylicious Vanilla Cake

DF LF

MAKES A 20CM (8 INCH) ROUND CAKE

groundnut oil, for greasing

6 medium eggs

190g (6¾oz) golden caster sugar

2 teaspoons vanilla bean paste

190g (6¾oz) plain flour, sifted

TO SERVE

200g (7oz) Fruit Compote
  (see page 19)

1 quantity of Italian Meringue
  (see page 188)

TOP TIP

To add more flavour to the cake, add the zest of 1 orange before adding the flour.

1 Preheat the oven to 160°C/gas 3. Grease and line the base and sides of 3 x 20cm (8 inch) round sandwich tins with non-stick baking parchment.

2 In a large bowl, whisk the eggs with the caster sugar and the vanilla bean paste in a heatproof bowl set over a pan of barely simmering water just until the sugar dissolves and reaches a temperature of 40–45°C (104–113°F) – check with a thermometer or your fingers – it should feel like a hot bath.

3 Remove from the heat and transfer to an electric mixer. Continue to whisk at maximum speed for 15 minutes until the batter cools and thickens and triples in size.

4 Add the flour, 2 tablespoons at a time, and gently fold in with a metal spoon or rubber spatula until fully combined. This will help to avoid lumps without overworking the sponge.

5 Transfer the batter to the prepared tins and bake for 25–30 minutes until risen, golden brown and springs back when pressed.

6 Transfer to a wire rack. Leave the cake to cool for 5 minutes in the tin, then turn out and leave to cool completely.

7 To serve, place the base on a cake plate, and spread with half the Compote. Fill a large piping bag with an open star nozzle and fill with the Italian Meringue. Hand pipe one-third of the meringue in a large circle from the centre outwards. Repeat with the next layer of sponge. Once the final layer of sponge is in place, finish with the Italian Meringue. Use a blowtorch to colour and caramelize the meringue on the top layer.

Best eaten fresh on the day it is made. Not suitable for freezing.

Not so much 'Death by Chocolate' as 'Died and Gone to Heaven Chocolate' cake. There is a real trend towards gluten-free baking for those with an allergy or intolerance to wheat, or those simply wishing to cut down. Just because something is gluten free shouldn't make it bland and boring. This is a gluten-free version of my ultimate chocolate truffle torte. As the cake has so little flour – this can be substituted with gluten-free flour or ground almonds. The hero is the melted chocolate in the cake itself. If the cake is just baked, then chilled well, it will be stable enough to handle and decorate. Leave the cake to come up to room temperature to serve and you will have an indulgent cake with a fudgy centre.

Ultimate Chocolate Truffle Cake (gluten free)

MAKES A 15CM (6 INCH) LAYERED CAKE

250g (9oz) unsalted butter, softened

350g (12oz) soft brown sugar

5 large eggs (or 6 medium eggs), beaten

200g (7oz) dark chocolate (70% cocoa solids), melted and cooled

140g (5oz) ground almonds

grated zest of 2 oranges (optional)

1 quantity of Buttercream (see page 38), omitting the raspberry powder

seasonal fruits and/or edible flowers, to decorate

FOR THE CHOCOLATE GANACHE:

250g (9oz) unsalted butter, diced

500g (1lb 2oz) dark chocolate (70% cocoa solids), broken into pieces

125ml (4fl oz) double cream

TOP TIPS:
- Alternatively, bake this quantity recipe mixture in a 20cm (8 inch) cake tin for 1 hour.
- Use the Chocolate Ganache to pour over cakes, blend with buttercream for cakes and cupcakes, or pipe shell and leaf decorations.
- Store the Buttercream in the refrigerator for up to 14 days but use at room temperature. Alternatively, buttercream can be frozen for up to 3 months, then defrosted at room temperature.

1 Preheat the oven to 150°C/ gas 2. Line the base and sides of 2 x 15cm (6 inch) round tins with non-stick baking parchment.

2 Cream the butter and sugar together until light and fluffy. Add the beaten eggs in a slow and steady stream. With the mixer still on medium speed, pour in the melted chocolate until fully combined. The batter should be mousse-like.

3 Fold in the ground almonds with a spatula or metal spoon until fully mixed. Spoon the batter into the prepared tins and level the surfaces. Bake for 45 minutes until risen with a crust that will wobble slightly when gently shaken. You cannot test with a knife for this cake – if it comes out clean the cake is overbaked.

4 Transfer the cake to a wire rack and cool for 15 minutes. Cover the surface with non-stick baking parchment and place in the refrigerator to chill before handling.

5 To make the ganache, put the butter and chocolate in a heatproof bowl and melt for 1–2 minutes in the microwave on high until all but melted. Bring the cream to the boil on the hob, then pour the cream over the butter and chocolate. Stir with a wooden spoon until fully melted and combined. Leave to cool slightly.

6 To make the Chocolate Buttercream used on this cake, blend half of the cooled Chocolate Ganache with the Buttercream – you can use more or less depending on how chocolatey you like it.

7 Trim the top of the completely chilled cakes with a serrated knife. Use a palette knife to spread one cake generously with ganache buttercream, then invert the other on top. Fill a piping bag with buttercream and snip 1–2cm (½–¾ inch) from the end. Starting at the bottom, pipe the buttercream around the cake working your way upwards to the top. This will

help protect the cake crumb and fill all the gaps.

8 Draw a cake scraper, held perpendicular and straight, around the side of the cake, in one smooth, controlled movement. Spread the buttercream on top of the cake with a palette knife. Chill for about 30 minutes until set.

9 Fill a piping bag with warm, chocolate ganache and snip 5mm (¼ inch) from the end. Drizzle the ganache around the top edge of the cake first to control the drips down the sides. Fill in the top of the cake with warm ganache using a cranked handle palette knife. Leave to set at room temperature for 30 minutes before decorating with fresh berries and edible flowers.

This cake keeps well at room temperature, uncovered, for up to 7 days. Only refrigerate if the cake is decorated with fresh fruits but serve at room temperature. Suitable for freezing.

CHOCOLATE GANACHE

CHOCOLATE BUTTERCREAM

6

ASSEMBLING THE CAKE

7　　　　　**8**

9

Gluten-free flour
chocolate cake

Plain wheat flour
chocolate cake

Trio of chocolate cakes – the chocolate cake recipe on the previous page can be made with plain flour, gluten-free flour or ground almonds. All will work well.

- The gluten-free flour will give a slightly drier cake with a more crumbly, grittier texture.
- The cake made with ground almonds will be the most moist but equally, very rich flavour.
- The wheat flour provides a truffle texture, less rich than the ground almonds.

Ground almond chocolate cake

This chocolate cake delivers a classic combination of chocolate and orange. Serve this showstopper for a special celebration as it has a higher proportion of butter and sugar to some of the other recipes. By making your own soft orange curd and chocolate Swiss meringue buttercream – the filling and frosting will have less sugar than most ready-bought preserves and regular buttercream.

Layered Chocolate Orange Cake

MAKES A 20CM (8 INCH) LAYERED ROUND CAKE

375g (13oz) unsalted butter, plus extra for greasing

200g (7oz) golden caster sugar

175g (6oz) light brown sugar

6 large eggs (weighing about 375g/13oz)

320g (11¼oz) self-raising flour

2 teaspoons baking powder

65g (2¼oz) cocoa powder

grated zest of 3 oranges

60ml (2½fl oz) whole milk

1 quantity Orange Curd (see page 18), for the filling

50g (1¾oz) dark chocolate (70% cocoa solids), for making decorations

6–8 physallis, to decorate

FOR THE CHOCOLATE SWISS MERINGUE

½ quantity of Swiss Meringue Buttercream (see page 162), made without the blackcurrant powder

225g (8oz) melted cooled dark chocolate (70% cocoa solids)

1 Preheat the oven to 170°C/gas 3. Grease and line the base and sides of 3 x 20cm (8 inch) round sandwich cake tins.

2 Place the butter and sugars in a large bowl and mix until light and fluffy. Add the beaten eggs a little at a time until fully incorporated. Sift the flour, baking powder and cocoa together and fold into the cake mixture. Stir in the orange zest and milk.

3 Divide the batter evenly between the prepared tins and level the surface with the back of a spoon. Bake for 25 minutes until the cakes are baked, beginning to come away from the side of the tin and spring back when pressed gently.

4 Remove from the oven and transfer to a wire rack. Leave the cake to cool in the tin for 5 minutes before turning out to cool completely.

Continued overleaf...

5 Make the Swiss Meringue Buttercream as instructed on page 164, then gently pour in the cooled, melted chocolate and stir until smooth. Spoon the buttercream into a piping bag.

6 For the chocolate decorations, melt the chocolate in a bowl in the microwave and pour into a piping bag. Snip the end and hand pipe decorations onto a chilled baking sheet lined with non-stick baking parchment. Leave to set.

7 Chill the cakes, then trim each one to level. Cut each cake in half with a serrated knife. Place one layer on a plate and spread with one-third of the Orange Curd.

8 Place a layer of sponge on top and spread with buttercream. Repeat until you have 6 layers

of sponge with 5 layers of filling, starting and ending with a layer of Orange Curd. Skim coat the cake with the buttercream and chill.

9 Starting at the base, pipe a vertical column of large pearls, then draw across each horizontally with a small palette knife as shown. Repeat with the next column of pearls covering the tails of the previous column. Continue all the way round the cake until it is fully decorated.

10 Peel off the set chocolate decorations from the baking parchment and position them on the top of the cake and decorate with physalis.

Store for up to 3 days, uncovered, in the refrigerator. Serve at room temperature. Not suitable for freezing.

CHOCOLATE SWISS MERINGUE

5

6

DECORATING THE CAKE

9

This chocolate gateau is made up of layers of chocolate genoise sponge with very little fat. I have layered it with black cherry jam and kirsch Chantilly cream to round off the flavour. By reducing the butter, this cake will have much lower fat than a regular chocolate buttercream cake. Nonetheless impressive, opt for this healthier version of a classic combination and decorate with fresh black cherries.

Lower Fat Chocolate Cherry Cream Cake

MAKES A 20CM (8 INCH) LAYERED CAKE

40g (1½oz) melted butter, plus extra for greasing

6 medium eggs

190g (6¾oz) golden caster sugar

150g (5½oz) plain flour

45g (1½oz) cocoa powder

500g (1lb 2oz) black cherry jam

875g (1lb 14oz) fresh black cherries, stoned

FOR THE CRÈME CHANTILLY

450ml (16fl oz) double cream

110g (4oz) caster sugar

3 tablespoons kirsch OR 1 tablespoon vanilla bean paste

1 Preheat the oven to 180°C/gas 4. Grease and line the base and sides of 4 x 20cm (8 inch) round sandwich tins with non-stick baking parchment.

2 Place the eggs with the caster sugar in a large heatproof bowl over a pan of barely simmering water and whisk with an electric hand whisk until tripled in size, pale and leaves a ribbon trail. Remove from the heat.

3 Sift together the flour and cocoa powder into the batter and gently fold in with a metal spoon or rubber spatula until fully combined. Drizzle in the melted butter.

4 Transfer the batter to the prepared tin and bake for 12–15 minutes until risen and springs back when pressed. Do not overbake as the sponge will be dry. Transfer to a wire rack. Leave the cake to cool for 5 minutes, then turn out and leave to cool completely.

5 To make the crème Chantilly, whip the cream, sugar and kirsch or vanilla together until voluminous and firm but still glossy. Be careful not to overwhip.

6 To serve, cut the sponges in half horizontally with a serrated knife. Place one sponge on a cake plate and spread with one-third of the cherry jam, then one-third of the kirsch crème Chantilly.

7 Repeat with the other sponges, jam and cream finishing with the final sponge. Decorate with fresh black cherries.

Store for up to 3 days, uncovered, in the refrigerator. Serve at room temperature. Not suitable for freezing.

The red velvet cake originates from the southern states of America and gains its name from the natural red coloured anthocyanin released when the cocoa reacts with the buttermilk and vinegar. Modern cocoa processing has removed this reaction making it necessary to add red colouring to achieve the same universally recognized colour. I have chosen to add natural beetroot powder to create the red hue. This cake is visually exciting, with a subtle chocolate flavour and velvety sweet cream cheese frosting. I guarantee you the sense of achievement this cake will give you once made is well worth the effort. A super and special cake to celebrate many occasions – for family, friends and colleagues.

Natural Red Velvet Cake

MAKES A 20CM (8 INCH) LAYERED ROUND CAKE

200g (7oz) unsalted butter, at room temperature, plus extra for greasing

420g (15oz) plain flour

75g (2¾oz) cocoa powder

50g (1¾oz) beetroot powder

375g (13oz) golden caster sugar

3 eggs, beaten

1½ teaspoons vanilla extract

335ml (11fl oz) buttermilk

1½ teaspoons bicarbonate of soda

1½ teaspoons white distilled vinegar

2 quantities of Cream Cheese Frosting (see page 134), made with vanilla extract added to taste instead of the orange zest

FOR THE SUGAR-FROSTED ROSE PETALS

a handful of red rose petals, washed and patted dry

1 egg white, lightly whisked

caster sugar, for sprinkling

1 First, make the sugar-frosted rose petals the day before you will be baking your cake. Use a pastry or clean paintbrush to brush the rose petals with egg white – it is important the egg white is lightly whisked and it is only the froth that is used when frosting fruits and petals. Sprinkle with caster sugar, shake off the excess and leave the petals to dry overnight on absorbent kitchen paper.

 TOP TIP
You can also frost herbs and small berries (redcurrant, blueberries) in the same way.

1

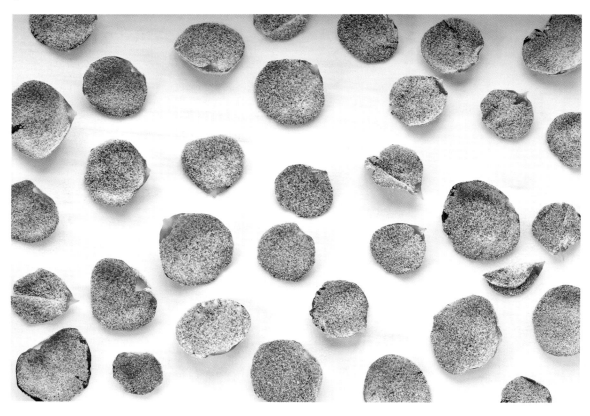

2 When you are ready to bake, preheat the oven to 180°C/gas 4. Grease 4 x 20cm (8 inch) sandwich tins and line with non-stick baking parchment.

3 Combine the flour, cocoa and beetroot powder in a large bowl and set aside.

4 In another large bowl, cream the butter and sugar together. Slowly whisk in the beaten eggs, then the vanilla extract.

5 Start adding the flour mixture to the butter mixture in batches, whisking well but slowly after each addition. The cake mixture will be thick. Add the buttermilk and stir until smooth.

6 Working quickly, combine the bicarbonate of soda and vinegar in a small bowl, then fold it into the cake mixture. Once incorporated, divide the batter between the prepared cake tins.

7 Bake for 25 minutes or until a skewer inserted in the centre comes out clean. Remove and cool slightly in the tin before turning out onto a wire rack to cool completely.

8 Trim the cakes so they are level. Fill a large piping bag with a plain nozzle and the Cream Cheese Frosting. Place the first cake on a cake stand or plate and pipe large pearls of frosting on the top, starting at the outside and working your way inwards. Top with the next layer of cake and repeat until all the layers are lined up and the top is fully decorated with frosting. Decorate with frosted rose petals.

Store for 3 days, uncovered, in the refrigerator. Not suitable for freezing.

6

Lemon Meringue Chiffon – a real showstopper – layered with homemade lemon curd and decorated with Italian meringue and fresh fruit.

Chiffon or angel cake is the lightest of all the sponge cakes –
using the fabulous aeration properties of egg white to create a
cake with volume. By nature, it has no, or very little fat, making
it a good choice for those who are looking to reduce their fat
intake. Don't feel too virtuous though – this cake is layered with
a homemade lemon curd and smothered in Italian meringue.

**MAKES A 25CM (10 INCH)
ROUND CAKE**

FOR THE CHIFFON

270g (9¾oz) plain flour

300g (10½oz) golden caster sugar

2¼ teaspoons baking powder

120ml (4fl oz) sunflower oil

7 large egg yolks

180ml (6fl oz) whole milk

9 large egg whites (weighing
    about 315g/11oz)

½ teaspoon cream of tartar

2 teaspoons vanilla bean paste

grated zest of 2 lemons

1 quantity of Lemon Curd (see
    page 18), for the filling

fresh strawberries and
    raspberries and roasted
    chopped pistachios, to
    decorate

FOR THE ITALIAN MERINGUE

300g (10½oz) golden caster sugar

25g (1oz) liquid glucose

65ml (2½fl oz) water

4 medium egg whites (weighing
    about 140g/5oz)

Lemon Meringue Chiffon

TO MAKE THE CHIFFON:

1 Preheat the oven to 170°C/gas 3. Mix together the flour, 150g
(5½oz) of the sugar and the baking powder. In a separate bowl,
whisk together the oil, egg yolks and milk.

2 Whisk the egg whites on high speed until frothy. Add the cream
of tartar and vanilla bean paste and continue whisking to soft peak
stage. Gradually add the remaining sugar, 1 teaspoon at a time,
until you have a wonderfully light, aerated, velvety meringue. Add
the flour mixture to the egg yolk mixture and use a balloon whisk
until combined. Stir through the lemon zest.

3 Use a rubber spatula or metal spoon to fold in one-third of the
meringue (foam) into the flour batter. Gently fold in the remaining
foam in 2 batches using a large metal spoon. It is important that the
batter and foam are evenly distributed and thoroughly mixed at this
stage to ensure an even baked chiffon.

4 Pour the batter into a 25cm (10 inch) tube pan which MUST NOT be
lined or greased – and leave a head space of 2.5cm (1 inch). Bake
for 50–60 minutes until risen, golden and a knife inserted comes
away clean. Remove the cake from the oven and immediately turn
it upside down to cool (see Tip, page 189).

Continued overleaf...

Continued overleaf...

VARIATION

*Orange and Pistachio Chiffon – replace the lemon zest with
orange zest and stir in 150g (5½oz) lightly chopped roasted
pistachios to the batter before baking. Cut and spread with
Orange Curd (see page 18) and dress with fresh strawberries
and chopped pistachios.*

TOP TIPS:

- Depending on how warm the room is, and how well the batter has aerated – you may not need to use all the cake batter – don't be tempted to fill the tin to the top – this cake has a wonderful lift during baking, and overfilling the tin will only cause the batter to rise up and spill over in the oven.

- Do not be tempted to line or grease this tin – the secret to a great chiffon is relying on the batter being able to literally claw its way up the outside and inside walls of the tin.
- Cooling the cake in the tin upside down will ensure the cake sets in its wonderfully risen position, allowing the steam to escape and preventing a soggy chiffon. Rest assured, the cake will NOT drop out!

4

PREPARE THE ITALIAN MERINGUE:

5 Measure the sugar, glucose and water into a saucepan and heat over a medium-high heat, stirring gently. Place a sugar thermometer in the sugar solution and stop stirring when the solution reaches 80°C (176°F). Continue heating without stirring until the temperature reaches 110°C (230°F).

6 Put the egg whites in a clean bowl attached to an electric whisk and start whisking on full speed. As the syrup reaches 119°C (246°F), remove the pan from the heat and, with the egg whites still on full speed, add the syrup to the egg whites in a slow, steady stream. Once all the syrup has been added, whisk until the meringue has cooled. The meringue is now ready to use straight away.

5

6

TO ASSEMBLE:

7 Run a knife around the inside of the tin to loosen the cake and carefully remove from the tin. Trim the base and place on a cake stand.

8 Slice the cake horizontally into 3 layers and spread each layer with the Lemon Curd.

9 Fill a large piping bag with an open rosette nozzle (195C)

and spoon one-third of the meringue into the bag.

10 Use a palette knife to paddle the remaining meringue over the top and sides of the cake until the surface is completely coated.

11 Hand pipe shells around the base of the chiffon and rosettes on the top of the chiffon in a circular motion.

Use a blow torch to gently caramelize and colour the Italian Meringue, taking care not to singe the peaks of the meringue. Decorate with the fresh fruit and roasted pistachios.

Store for up to 3 days, uncovered, in the refrigerator but serve at room temperature. Not suitable for freezing.

7

8

10

Gingerbread Cake with Cream Cheese Frosting

Ginger cake is a homely favourite. Melting the ingredients together means the cake will be wonderfully moist and guaranteed results time after time. Molasses has no fat and no cholesterol and is a good source of both calcium and iron, for healthy bones, blood and energy. The cake itself is dairy free and I have used a cream cheese frosting, which will be naturally lower in fat than buttercream.

MAKES A 23CM (9 INCH) ROUND CAKE

groundnut oil, for greasing

170ml (6fl oz) boiling water

½ teaspoon bicarbonate of soda

150g (5½oz) molasses

170g (6oz) golden caster sugar

240g (8½oz) plain flour

2 teaspoons ground ginger

1 teaspoon ground cinnamon

¼ teaspoon ground nutmeg

a pinch of ground cloves

½ teaspoon baking powder

80ml (2¾fl oz) sunflower oil

2 large eggs

½ quantity of Cream Cheese Frosting (see page 134)

frosted cranberries or redcurrants and mint leaves (see page 184), to decorate

1 Preheat the oven to 170°C/gas 3. Grease and line the base of a 23cm (9 inch) springform tin.

2 In a large heatproof bowl, blend the boiling water with the bicarbonate of soda. Add the molasses and sugar and whisk well until the sugars dissolve. Set aside.

3 In a large mixing bowl, sift together all the remaining dry ingredients.

4 Stir the oil and eggs into the molasses mixture. Tip the flour into the molasses mixture and stir with a balloon whisk until fully incorporated and smooth.

5 Pour the batter into the prepared tin and bake for 30–35 minutes, until a knife inserted in the centre comes out clean.

6 Transfer the cake to a wire rack and leave to cool in the tin for 10 minutes. Run a knife around the tin before removing the ring, then leave the cake to cool completely.

7 To serve, place the cake on a plate and spread the Cream Cheese Frosting over the top with a palette knife. Decorate with frosted cranberries or redcurrants and mint leaves.

Store for up to 3 days, uncovered, in the refrigerator but serve at room temperature. Not suitable for freezing.

LEFT This dark chocolate and coconut cake is dairy and oil free.
RIGHT Dairy-free raspberry and coconut loaf cake with a hint of lime.

Loaf cakes are quick to prepare and easy to slice. This recipe combines dark chocolate with coconut for a tasty, dairy-free, oil-free cake. Coconut milk offers a delicious, authentic taste and richness to the baked cake. With 20% fat, it is much lower than butter or margarine at 80%.

Dairy-free Chocolate & Coconut Loaf

MAKES 1 LARGE LOAF CAKE

400ml (14fl oz) full-fat coconut milk

175g (6oz) desiccated coconut

groundnut oil, for greasing

225g (8oz) golden caster sugar

2 eggs, beaten (weighing about 100g/3½oz)

2 teaspoons vanilla bean paste

230g (8¼oz) self-raising flour

75g (2¾oz) dairy-free dark chocolate (70% cocoa solids), grated (or 50g/1¾oz cocoa nibs)

15g (½oz) toasted coconut flakes, to decorate

FOR THE DAIRY-FREE CHOCOLATE ICING

170g (6oz) dairy-free dark chocolate (70% cocoa solids), broken into pieces

90ml (3fl oz) water

220g (8oz) golden icing sugar

1 In a mixing bowl, pour the coconut milk over the desiccated coconut and leave, covered, for 10 minutes to absorb. Preheat the oven to 170°C/gas 3. Grease and line the base and sides of a 900g (2lb) loaf tin.

2 Add the sugar, eggs and vanilla to the soaked coconut and stir with a metal spoon. Sift in the flour and fold in the chocolate.

3 Spoon the batter into the prepared tin and bake for 1 hour and 20–30 minutes until golden brown and a knife inserted in the centre comes out clean. Remove from the oven and transfer to a wire rack. Leave the cake to cool in the tin for 10 minutes, then carefully turn out and leave to cool completely.

4 To make the icing, place the chocolate and water in a small heavy-based saucepan and heat gently until melted and smooth. Remove from the heat and beat in the icing sugar until the chocolate icing is smooth and all the lumps have gone. To decorate, re-heat the chocolate icing if needed, then brush the icing over the top of the loaf. Scatter with the coconut.

Store for up to 3 days, uncovered, in the refrigerator but serve at room temperature. Not suitable for freezing.

VARIATIONS

RASPBERRY & COCONUT – replace the chocolate with 180g (6oz) fresh raspberries and add the grated zest and juice of 1 lime. Top with 4 tablespoons raspberry jam and scatter with desiccated coconut. Alternatively, substitute the fresh raspberries with any summer berries – choosing the smaller strawberries, or cutting into quarters. Similarly the jam could be replaced with strawberry, blackcurrant or apricot. Lemons, limes and oranges can all be used to complement the flavour of this cake.

4

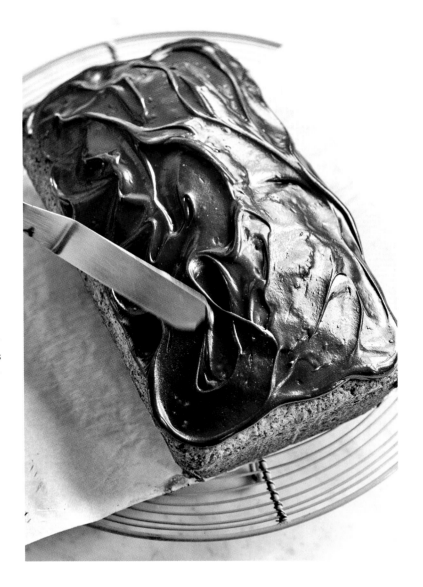

TOP TIPS
- Coconut milk tends to separate so shake well before opening the can, or decant the entire contents and stir thoroughly before measuring.
- Chill the cake to make it easier to slice and serve.

This loaf cake combines oil and Greek-style yogurt for a moist, butter-free loaf. I have added subtle flavours of lemon, honey and pistachio for a Mediterranean flavour. Add cardamom and orange for a more pronounced flavour. Greek-style yogurt is less than 10 percent fat and is unsweetened, making this a healthier choice for a weekend bake. The gluten-free polenta will add colour and texture.

Lemon, Pistachio & Honey Loaf Cake

MAKES 1 LARGE LOAF CAKE

160ml (5½fl oz) sunflower oil, plus extra for greasing

365ml (13fl oz) full-fat Greek-style yogurt

3 large eggs

2 tablespoons (50g/1¾oz) clear honey (I used orange blossom or acacia)

1 teaspoon vanilla bean paste

grated zest 2 lemons

juice of 1 lemon

250g (9oz) self-raising flour

60g (2¼oz) polenta

250g (9oz) golden caster sugar

½ teaspoon bicarbonate of soda

90g (3¼oz) roasted and finely chopped pistachios

FOR THE LEMON SYRUP

45ml (1¾fl oz) lemon juice

65g (2½oz) golden caster sugar

1 Preheat the oven to 170°C/gas 3. Grease and line a 900g (2lb) loaf tin.

2 Place the oil, yogurt, eggs, honey, vanilla and lemon zest in a large mixing bowl and beat until well combined. Add the lemon juice, flour, polenta, sugar, bicarbonate of soda and 50g (1¾oz) of the pistachios and beat on a slow speed until you have a smooth, well combined batter. Pour into the prepared tin.

3 Bake for 45 minutes until risen, golden brown and a knife inserted in the centre comes out clean.

4 Remove the cake from the oven and transfer to a wire rack. Leave the cake to cool in the tin for 10 minutes before turning out to cool completely.

5 To make the syrup, heat the lemon juice and sugar together until dissolved and reduced to a syrup.

6 Place the cake on a plate and drizzle with the lemon syrup. Decorate with the remaining chopped pistachios.

Store for up to 3 days, uncovered, in the refrigerator but serve at room temperature. Not suitable for freezing.

These mini loaves are deliciously nutritious – with dates, banana, raisins and pecans. I have used polenta so the cakes are gluten free and with no butter or oil, the cake is dairy free and fat free.

Fruity Date & Tea Loaves

MAKES 6 MINI TEA LOAVES

250g (9oz) Medjool dates, stoned
   and ready to eat

200ml (7fl oz) boiling water

2 ripe bananas (about 140g/5oz)

80g (3oz) pecans, chopped

200g (7oz) raisins

200g (7oz) dried cherries

100g (3½oz) fine polenta

2 teaspoons mixed spice

2 teaspoons baking powder
   (gluten-free)

60ml (2¼fl oz) strong brewed tea

2 large egg whites (weighing
   about 70g/2½oz)

TO DECORATE

20g (¾oz) pecan halves

50g (1¾oz) banana chips

1 Preheat the oven to 170°C/gas 3. Lay 6 mini tea loaf cases on a baking tray.

2 Put the dates in a saucepan with the boiling water and simmer until the dates have softened. Drain the liquid into a jug and transfer the dates to a food processor or blender. Add the bananas and 100ml (3½fl oz) of the date liquid. Blitz until smooth.

3 In a separate bowl, mix together the chopped pecans, dried fruit, polenta, spice and baking powder. Add the date purée and the tea and stir until combined.

4 Whisk the egg whites to the soft peak stage, then fold into the cake batter in 3 batches. Divide the batter between the mini loaf cases and decorate with the pecans and banana chips.

5 Bake for 25 minutes until golden, firm to the touch and a knife inserted in the centre comes out clean. Remove the cakes from the oven and transfer to a wire rack. Leave the cakes to cool in the cases for 10 minutes before turning out to cool completely.

Store for up to 3 days, uncovered, in the refrigerator but serve at room temperature. Not suitable for freezing.

VARIATION
Bake this batter in a 450g (1lb) loaf tin for 1 hour for one larger loaf cake.

TOP TIP
Medjool dates are soft dates that are large, sweet, moist, meaty and firm textured. They are likely to be more expensive but offer a superior flavour and texture. Deglet Noor dates are more widely available and are semi-dry. They have a firmed flesh and will need more liquid to soften them. They are generally less expensive than Medjool dates.

LEFT Quick and easy banana loaf.
RIGHT Pumpkin and poppy seed loaf
with lemon drizzle icing.

What do you do with all those bananas when they are overripe and the skin is blackened? Bake a banana loaf cake! This blackening indicates a natural ripening process where the starch is broken down to its simple sugars – the banana softens and tastes sweeter. Do not be tempted to put bananas in the refrigerator – this will cause a 'cold shock' whereby the bananas will turn black but the ripening process cannot occur. This simple loaf cake is perfect as an introduction to baking, and ideal to make with children. With added minerals and fibre the cake is perfect for breakfast, packed lunches and picnics.

Quick Banana Cake

MAKES 1 SMALL LOAF CAKE

125g (4½oz) unsalted butter

150g (5½oz) soft light brown sugar

2–3 very ripe bananas, mashed with a fork (weighing about 200g/7oz)

1 teaspoon vanilla bean paste

1 large egg, beaten

190g (6¾oz) self-raising flour

60ml (2¼fl oz) whole milk

demerara sugar, for sprinkling

1 Preheat the oven to 170°C/gas 3. Line the base and sides of a 450g (1lb) loaf tin.

2 Melt the butter and sugar together in a saucepan over a medium heat. Remove from the heat, leave to cool for 5 minutes, then add the mashed bananas and vanilla. Add the beaten egg and stir well. Stir in the flour, followed by the milk.

3 Pour into the prepared tin, sprinkle with a tablespoon of demerara sugar and bake for 35–40 minutes until risen, golden and a knife inserted in the centre comes out clean.

4 Transfer to a wire rack. Leave to cool for 10 minutes in the tin, then turn out and leave to cool completely.

Store at room temperature, covered loosely with non-stick baking parchment or waxed paper and foil and consume within 3 days. Not suitable for freezing.

VARIATION
Add cinnamon, a handful of raisins or sunflower seeds to the loaf for added flavour, nutrition and texture. Experiment to find your favourite additions.

We are surrounded by pumpkin bakes around the time of Thanksgiving. This easy loaf cake is a great introduction to baking with pumpkin – either with a can of pumpkin purée or making your own from scratch. This loaf is quick and easy to make, has less fat than a traditional pumpkin pie and can be made to share with the office, family and friends to wish them all Happy Holidays. Not that we really need an excuse – this loaf is delicious and nutritious all year round! For that, I give thanks!

Pumpkin, Poppy Seed & Lemon Loaf

MAKES 1 SMALL LOAF CAKE

60ml (2¼fl oz) whole milk

1 large egg

225g (8oz) canned pumpkin purée

175g (6oz) self-raising flour

½ teaspoon baking powder

¼ teaspoon bicarbonate of soda

2 teaspoons ground cinnamon

1 teaspoon ground ginger

150g (5½oz) soft light brown sugar

50g (1¾oz) unsalted butter

1 tablespoon poppy seeds

grated zest 2 lemon

1 quantity of Lemon Drizzle (see page 142), to decorate

1 Preheat the oven to 180°C/gas 4. Line the base and sides of a 450g (1lb) loaf tin. Add the milk and egg to the pumpkin purée and stir until smooth.

2 Sift the flour, raising agents, spices and sugar together, then rub in the butter until it resembles fine breadcrumbs.

3 Stir the dry crumbs into the pumpkin mixture and stir until just mixed. Stir in the poppy seeds and lemon zest.

4 Spoon the batter into the prepared tin and bake for 45 minutes until risen, golden and a knife inserted in the centre comes out clean. Transfer to a wire rack. Leave to cool for 10 minutes in the tin, then turn out and leave to cool completely.

5 Pour the Lemon Drizzle over the cooled loaf to finish.

Store at room temperature, covered loosely with non-stick baking parchment or waxed paper and foil and consume within 3 days. Not suitable for freezing.

Meringues

'If you are rich, you have lovely cars, and jars full of flowers, and books in rows, and a wireless, and the best sort of gramophone and meringues for supper.'

WINIFRED HOLTBY, ENGLISH NOVELIST AND JOURNALIST 1898–1935

Gluten free, fat free and wonderfully light and simple to make, meringues offer a delicious versatility in baking. In this chapter, I have included individual meringues that can be decorated, dressed and deliciously devoured, as well as impressive pavlova and layered meringue for your showstopper celebrations. Simply served with fresh fruit and lightly whipped cream, these recipes are certain to be crowd pleasers!

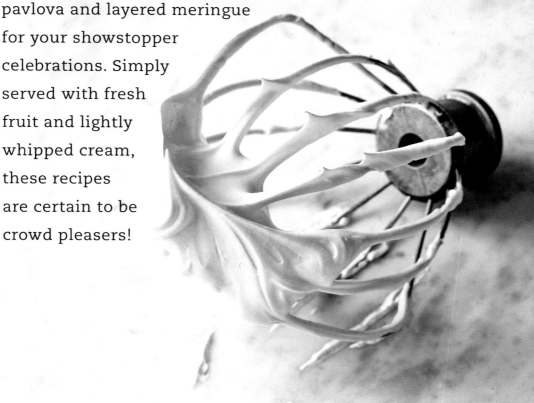

Meringues are by nature fat free, dairy free and gluten free –
made with high protein egg white and unrefined sugar. Adding
the fresh roasted nuts will ramp up the flavour and provide
added texture and nutrition. I like to roast, roughly chop and
add the hazelnuts at the time of making to ensure maximum
freshness and have sandwiched the gateau with fresh cream and
fruits (with an optional passion fruit curd). This is an impressive
gateau that is actually a lot lighter than you think, making it the
perfect centrepiece for a special occasion with less calories than
many other cakes or desserts.

Tropical Hazelnut Meringue

GF

SERVES 8

groundnut oil, for greasing

115g (4oz) hazelnuts

5 large egg whites

250g (9oz) golden caster sugar

½ teaspoon distilled white
    vinegar

1 teaspoon vanilla extract

400g (14oz) fresh mango

400ml (14fl oz) double cream

4–6 tablespoons Passion Fruit
    Curd (see page 18)

grated zest and juice of 1 lemon

fresh edible flowers, to decorate

1 Preheat the oven to 170°C/gas 3. Draw a 20cm (8 inch) circle on 2 sheets of non-stick baking parchment and use them to line 2 greased baking trays.

2 Place the hazelnuts on a baking sheet and roast in the oven for 10–15 minutes until golden. Remove from the oven and place in a clean tea towel. Gather the corners up and rub to remove the husks. Roughly chop in a grinder, food processor or blender, then reserve 1 tablespoon for decoration.

3 Whisk the egg whites until stiff but not dry. Add the sugar gradually. Whisk in the vinegar and vanilla, then fold in the chopped nuts. Spread the meringue into the circles on the prepared baking sheets and level the surfaces. Bake for 30 minutes until firm to the touch. Remove from the oven and leave in the tins to cool completely. Turn out onto a wire rack and leave to cool completely.

4 Biltz the mango in a food processor or blender to make a purée. Whip the cream until soft and just holding its shape. Stir in 4 tablespoons mango purée.

5 Place the base meringue on a serving plate, spread with the half the mango cream. Drizzle with 2–3 tablespoons Passion Fruit Curd, then place the other meringue on top. Top with the remaining cream and curd and dress with chopped hazelnuts and fresh edible flowers.

6 Mix the remaining mango purée with the lemon juice and zest to taste and pour into a serving jug. Chill the meringue gateau and sauce in the refrigerator overnight and serve in large wedges with the sauce poured over.

Store for up to 3 days, uncovered, in the refrigerator but serve at room temperature. Not suitable for freezing.

2

3

5

Banana, Coconut & Caramel Pavlova

GF

SERVES 12

6 large egg whites at room
   temperature

280g (10oz) golden caster sugar

1 teaspoon distilled white vinegar

½ teaspoon cream of tartar

85g (3oz) desiccated coconut

FOR THE TOPPING

350ml (12fl oz) whipping cream,
   whipped

3 ripe bananas

½ quantity Salted Caramel
   (see page 106) – or make
   unsalted if preferred

25g (1oz) desiccated coconut

> ## TOP TIP
> To toast the coconut,
> spread on a tray and bake
> in the oven at 180°C/gas 4
> for 5 minutes, then leave
> to cool.

If you are a lover of banoffee pie but looking for a healthier option, this is the perfect bake to consider. The gluten-free and dairy-free coconut meringue is filled with fresh cream, sliced banana and drizzled with caramel that can also be served on the side.

1 Preheat the oven to 180°C/gas 4. Draw a 25cm (10 inch) circle on a sheet of non-stick baking parchment and use it to line a baking tray.

2 Beat the egg whites until stiff peaks, but not dry and add the sugar 1 tablespoon at a time until stiff and shiny. Add the vinegar and cream of tartar and stir in the desiccated coconut.

3 Spread the meringue into the circle on the prepared tray and make an indentation in the centre with the back of a spoon.

4 Transfer to the oven, immediately reduce the temperature to 120°C/gas ¼–½ and bake for 1 hour 30 minutes. Turn off the oven, open the door slightly and leave the meringue to cool completely in the oven.

5 Place the meringue on a large plate, pile with whipped cream and slice over the fresh, ripe bananas. Drizzle the caramel over the top and sprinkle with toasted coconut. Serve additional caramel sauce on the side.

The meringue can be made up to 3 days in advance and stored in an airtight container at room temperature. Once filled, it should be consumed the same day, within 4 hours. Not suitable for freezing.

Raspberry & Rose Meringues

GF

MAKES 24 INDIVIDUAL MERINGUES

280g (10oz) golden caster sugar

6 large egg whites (room temperature)

½ teaspoon cream of tartar

1 teaspoon distilled white vinegar

2 teaspoons rose water

4 teaspoons freeze-dried raspberry powder

FOR THE TOPPING

150ml (5fl oz) double cream

65g (2¼oz) raspberries

100g (3½oz) fresh redcurrants

1 tablespoon edible dried rose petals

1 Preheat the oven to 180°C/gas 4. Line a baking sheet with non-stick baking parchment. Place the sugar and egg whites in a large heatproof bowl over a pan of simmering water. Stir and heat until the temperature reaches 65°C (149°F). Remove from the heat, then whisk the meringue with the cream of tartar and vinegar until it cools and thickens. Stir in the rose water and raspberry powder.

2 Fill a piping bag with a large star nozzle and the meringue mixture and pipe rounds onto the prepared baking sheet.

3 Transfer to the oven, immediately reduce the temperature to 120°C/gas ¼–½ and bake for 45 minutes until dried on the top. Turn off the oven, open the door slightly and leave the meringues to cool completely in the oven.

4 To serve, whip the cream and fold in the raspberries. Spoon the cream onto each meringue and decorate with redcurrants and rose petals.

The addition of the raspberry powder means the meringues absorb moisture and go chewy really quickly, so they are best made and eaten on the same day. Not suitable for freezing.

Raspberry and rose have a wonderful synergy and the flavours are indicative of hazy summer days. These gluten-free treats feature pillowy meringues, paired with a fresh raspberry cream and are decorated with fresh fruit.

These dairy-free, gluten-free meringues are enhanced with cocoa, grated dark chocolate and pistachios for added flavour, texture and nutrition. I have chosen to fill these with a chocolate cream. For a completely dairy-free version, serve the meringue, fruit and chocolate in pretty, glass bowls with a non-dairy pourable cream.

Chocolate Pistachio Pavlova

 GF

MAKES 18 INDIVIDUAL MERINGUES

280g (10oz) golden caster sugar

6 large egg whites, at room temperature

1 teaspoon distilled white vinegar

½ teaspoon cream of tartar

50g (1¾oz) dark chocolate (70% cocoa solids), grated

45g (1½oz) cocoa powder

50g (1¾oz) chopped roasted pistachios

FOR THE TOPPING

140g (5oz) dark chocolate (70% cocoa solids), broken into pieces

70ml (2½fl oz) water

570ml (19fl oz) double cream

70g (2½oz) caster sugar

50g (1¾oz) chopped roasted pistachios, to decorate

1 Preheat the oven to 150°C/gas 2. Line a baking sheet with non-stick baking parchment.

2 Place the sugar and egg whites in a large heatproof bowl over a pan of simmering water. Whisk with a hand whisk until the temperature reaches 61–70°C (142–158°F). Transfer to an electric mixer, add the vinegar and cream of tartar and continue to whisk until the meringue is thick and white and reaches the stiff peak stage. Carefully fold in the chocolate, cocoa and 30g (1¼oz) of the pistachios.

3 Drop spoonfuls of meringue onto the baking sheet, leaving room for the meringues to spread. Use the back of a spoon to make a little indentation on the top and sprinkle with the remaining pistachios.

4 Transfer to the oven, immediately reduce the temperature to 100°C/gas ¼ and bake for 1 hour until dried on the top. Turn off the oven, open the door slightly and leave the meringues to cool completely in the oven.

5 Make the topping. Melt 110g (4oz) of the chocolate and the water together in a saucepan, then leave to cool. Start whisking the cream and sugar and as it thickens, add the melted chocolate. Continue whisking until the cream holds its shape. Fill each meringue with whipped chocolate cream.

6 Melt the remaining chocolate over a pan of simmering water or in the microwave, then place it in a piping bag. Drizzle the meringues with the melted chocolate and top with the chopped pistachios.

The meringues can be made up to 3 days in advance and stored in an airtight container at room temperature. Once filled, they should be consumed the same day, within 4 hours. Not suitable for freezing.

This dacquoise combines thinner layers of chewy almond meringue with fresh cream, apricot compote and gloriously crunchy almond praline. As a gluten-free cake this is truly decadent, visually enticing with so many textures.

Almond Dacquoise

GF

SERVES 12–16

5 egg whites, at room
    temperature

½ teaspoon cream of tartar

285g (10oz) golden caster sugar

110g (4oz) ground almonds

400ml (14fl oz) double cream

1 quantity of Praline (see page
    134), made with almonds
    instead of walnuts, roughly
    chopped, to decorate

FOR THE APRICOT PURÉE

225g (8oz) fresh apricots

golden caster sugar, to taste

grated zest and juice of 1 lemon

4–6 tablespoons water

1 Preheat the oven to 140°C/ gas 1. Line 3 baking trays with non-stick baking parchment, marking a 23cm (9 inch) diameter circle on each.

2 Whisk the egg whites with the cream of tartar until stiff peaks form, but not dry. Add the sugar 1 tablespoon at a time until stiff and shiny. Fold in the ground almonds

3 Divide the mixture between the prepared trays – fill a piping bag and pipe the outline of the circle, coming into the centre, as shown below.

4 Bake for 1 hour. Remove from the oven and cool slightly before removing the paper and transferring to a wire rack to cool completely.

5 To make the apricot purée, place the apricots in a saucepan with 2 tablespoons sugar, the lemon zest and juice and the water. Simmer until the fruit has softened. Place the fruit in a food processor or blender and blitz with enough liquid to make a purée. Cool and taste and adjust the sweetness to taste.

6 Whip the cream. Layer the meringues with the cream, drizzled apricot purée and roughly chopped praline.

The meringues can be made up to 3 days in advance and stored in an airtight container at room temperature. Once filled, they should be consumed the same day, within 4 hours. Not suitable for freezing.

Index

Stockists

It was key for me that this book should feature recipes made with store cupboard ingredients that are readily obtained from most supermarkets, grocery stores or online retailers. Ingredients that are recognizable, offer nutritional benefit and are there to enhance the recipe.

Amazon.co.uk is great for more obscure items like beetroot powder and freeze dried fruit powders – even tinned pumpkin!

For edible flowers I can recommend Maddoxfarmorganics.co.uk

Acknowledgements

It is not surprising that to have your cake and eat it there are many people deserving of a special mention.

Firstly to my publisher – Jacqui Small. We have worked together for over 10 years now. You are unsurpassed, admired and revered in the publishing world – for good reason. You publish books of the highest integrity, quality and creativity. You always inspire me to give my best, to make you proud of my books, that they are worthy of being featured in your library.

Huge thanks to the extended family at Jacqui Small and Quarto – always a pleasure to work with your team – Joe, Rebecca, Farmer Jon, Emma, Simon and Katy.

To the team at Barnes and Noble and Sterling publishing – you have given me a wonderful opportunity to publish a book with you after seeing me on stage at the Americas Cake and Sugarcraft Fair. I am a strong believer in making the most of every opportunity and maximizing these serendipitous moments. I hope this book is an enormous success for you too.

Special thanks to Ron Boire and Faith Ferguson for all their belief and support.

To all the team at Satin Ice – Kevin, Paul, Alan and Joyce – you make life sweeter every day.

To the dream team here in the UK – Penny and Abi – I can make it and bake it, but the magic comes from the two of you to make it all look so beautiful on the page and logical to read. Penny – please stop by any time for a slice of banana cake!

Peter Cassidy – what a pleasure and privilege to work with you – 'round and brown' with happy shared memories of GX and Little Venice. My best wishes to you and all the family. Thank you for bringing my bakes to life – and eating a few on the way!

Enormous thanks to David Birt and Emma Fuller – my Home Economists – your help and assistance was truly invaluable – and not just for Pop Master!

My agent – Fiona, Alison, Roz and Maclean at Limelight Management – thank you for all your unfaltering support. Can we turn this book into a TV series please?!!

Very special thanks to the team at William Edwards – James and William – for creating such beautiful Afternoon Tea fine bone china – the Mich Turner Collection – inspired by my cake designs. I am immensely proud of the collection and hope others will enjoy cakes from Have your cake and Eat It served on some of our china.